# INVITATION TO COMMUNE

*Charles Ray Goff*

# INVITATION
## TO COMMUNE

**ABINGDON PRESS**
NEW YORK • NASHVILLE

INVITATION TO COMMUNE

*Copyright © MCMLIX by Abingdon Press*

*Library of Congress Catalog Card Number: 59-5211*

*This book is dedicated
to my dear friend*

**HARGROVE  HUDSON**

# PREFACE

THIS LITTLE BOOK is an effort to put down the result of thinking about and experimenting with the sacrament of Communion in small churches and large. The experimentation grows out of dissatisfaction with the methods employed and the consequent moods created. If the service is formal and stilted, the result will be unnatural. What service in the church is as futile as Holy Communion if it fails to communicate? Conversely, is there any service comparable to the Communion when a congregation enters into it in a spirit of humility and with a hunger for righteousness?

Success can never be measured alone by the numbers who come, but if a church finds that the congregations are consistently larger on the Sundays when the Communion service is announced, this is an indication that some deep-felt need is being met. This book is written in the hope that it may add something to the growing appreciation of this central act of worship in our churches.

What can be more sterile than the use of a repetitious set of phrases, remote from actual experience and voiced in monotonous

7

tones, followed by an awkward act that loses all its mystery and holy suggestion by surroundings that destroy the imaginative approach? Given the same words and the same series of actions, this service can come alive and become a true means of grace.

There are details, minor in themselves but of great importance, such as the lighting, the ushering, the materials used, the posture, and a hundred others, which help to make or mar the beauty, the dignity, and the spiritual value of this service. A book larger than this could profitably be devoted to these details, which often become either major aids or obstacles.

I have chosen to limit this book to a discussion of the familiar phrases commonly used by the churches when inviting worshipers to Communion.

CHARLES R. GOFF

# CONTENTS

# CONTENTS

# ONE

## *On Repentance*

THE PHRASE "Ye that do truly and earnestly repent of your sins" is the opening part of the Communion invitation as found in many of the orders of worship of the church. Thirty years ago there was very little said about repentance, and the word "sin" was fading from our vocabulary. Today the situation is different. Two world wars have done something to our theology and to our views about man, his nature, and his need.

"We are all born Christians," said one prominent minister of that past age. "We can't get out of the Christian family unless we push our way out," was his way of putting it. But this sort of thinking has had to change. William Wordsworth's "trailing clouds of glory do we come from God, who is our home" would hardly do for a modern description of our origin.

We know now that we are capable of great evil, that we can easily revert to practices that are utterly selfish and cruel. We know now that we must repent—or perish. The hunger for reconciliation is evident in hearts everywhere. "Preach on forgiveness," said a desperate woman to me a few years ago. "I go from church to church, and nobody ever mentions it." That was an early and a wistful voice, but I hear more of that kind all the time.

The psychiatrist has seen the unfortunate effects of guilt feelings, but he has not often realized that many are the result of real sins. He has been skillful in helping people get rid of a load of imaginary guilt, but often helpless when confronted with real guilt which is the result of real sin. When we truly repent and are "heartily sorry for these our misdoings," we have a remedy which is not only soul-satisfying but definitely redemptive.

Repentance is hard to define. One can read books on the subject and get more and more confused. I think the story of Peter's denial and of his subsequent repentance is one of the best illustrations of true repentance. After Peter had denied his Lord, he was probably aware of his sin. A deep sense of guilt was upon him, but he kept insisting that he did not know who Christ was. When Christ turned and looked at Peter, however, there was in that look something that broke down all of Peter's defenses. He "went out, and wept bitterly." He had genuine sorrow—and it caused him to do something about the matter.

In thinking of repentance, we have to suppose, first of all, that there is some kind of judgment which we bring upon ourselves. We pass this judgment before the bar of our own court. We never repent of anything that we haven't first adjudged to be wrong, for it is impossible to repent of something we do not consider wrong. The sense of guilt, the feeling of it, is the result of the condemnation before the bar of our own souls. This is an essential step. I think we all have to face up to those things that at first do not seem to be evil at all. It is possible for a person to say to himself, over and over again, that a thing isn't wrong and thus to become quite convinced about it only because of a kind of self-hypnosis. But in this world, evil is evil, wrong is wrong, right is right; for it is an orderly world and as stable as the world of hydrogen and oxygen.

Pascal, in a mood of pessimism, claimed that right or wrong was all a matter of "jurisprudence"—or as he put it, "a matter of the meridian." What latitude were you born in?—What part of the world? In one country you could have one wife, and only one; in another, you had to have more than one if you were moral. Pascal implied that morality and right are merely matters of geography, as changeable as the weather. Of course, his was just a mood of pessimism; he knew better.

There are many people who justify their actions by an appeal to Pascal's mood. They try to make you feel that their actions are wrong only under certain circumstances, and that there is no absolute. A good deal of such thinking exists in many areas. "Things are relative," they say, "relative to the place, or the time, or the age, or the period." Now of course customs change—that is, they seem to shift with the part of the world you live in or the crowd you're in—but if there were no definite right or wrong, if there were nothing by which to measure our actions, we'd be helpless. In the physical world we have adopted weights and measures and have divided the world into standard time zones. In the moral universe, also, there must be something just as real.

Immanuel Kant was the man who said there were just two things that filled him with a sense of awe. One was the starry sky; and the other was the moral law in the heart of a human being. He had a big name for it—"the categorical imperative" —but he meant that there is something within a human being which says you *ought* or *ought not*—and this is the moral law. There is nobody who has not felt such a sense of moral right or wrong. True, some things are merely the result of our education. Some we got by association or from a distant past; others are simply accretions. But there's a core of right and wrong existing in the hearts of human beings which is as real as weights and measures and the many other things we feel so sure about in the physical world.

What part does repentance play in dealing with this law? When we've broken with something, when we've violated the law, when we've chosen the lesser instead of the higher, or when plain selfishness has gotten hold of our hearts and our own little concerns, it's then that we begin to realize we are less than we ought to be as human beings. There's something wrong within us and we can't be happy. We are "haunted night and day by some unloveliness." We are aware of something we have done or failed to do, and these thoughts will not let us alone. The offices of psychiatrists and counselors are filled all over America. There are long lists of people waiting for appointments. It would be most unfortunate if we had no answer to give to these distressed and distracted people. Surely an easy optimism is of little use. The view that the world, somehow or other, is getting over some of its foolish notions and that sin is the result of an inherited tendency, or that it can be cured by having a good look at it, is not enough. We know that repentance is not an old-fashioned notion belonging to the revival meeting era, but that it is a necessary part of the redemption of a soul.

Some time ago a group of us were studying together some of the great doctrines of the Christian faith, and we came to the doctrine of repentance. It was the first time I had become interested in this subject in the way that I am trying to describe here. It came about because one night a boy had stolen my car—

a brand-new one—from the Greyhound garage. He said he tried several and he liked mine better than any of the rest. In that, he used good judgment. It was one of the first cars with power steering, and since he had been in the penitentiary, he hadn't had a chance to try out the new cars. He said the car did bother him a little bit when he got it "above eighty."

The police called me on a Sunday morning, just before time to preach, to say they had the culprit, and would I come right out. I said, "No, I won't. You'll have to wait because I'm going to be preaching shortly." So they brought the boy downtown with the car. Before the case was completed, I found that I was almost worse off than the thief, because I had him on my hands. The judge said to me, "How would you sentence him? You tell me what I ought to do." I replied, "I don't know what you ought to do."

I heard the boy's story, a recounting of a series of unfortunate things. His father and mother were dead, and the poor fellow was left to shift for himself. I don't know how much of the story was true, but I could believe a good deal of it. Not having had a decent chance, he had got into one thing after another—a series of unhappy experiences—and you could understand every one of them.

There was a charge hanging over the boy down South. He had jumped parole and was to be returned to the penitentiary. Should I try to help him? I laid the whole story before my young adults, much more in detail than I'm giving it here, and said, "What would you do?" For one hour we had as vital a discussion as I ever engaged in. Everyone around that table felt that he was dealing with something alive. What would you do with this boy? Would you forgive him, or would you send him back to the penitentiary if you were the judge? By the time we got through with it, we had the answer. This was their judgment. It all depends, they said, on whether he had repented. If he had truly repented, and you knew that he had, you could certainly forgive. And I agree. I don't think it would have made any difference even if he had ruined the car. I don't normally get in such a state of forgiveness as that, but after I thought deeply about it I could see that I could forgive completely if I knew that he had truly repented. But how could I know?

Little by little we began to find out, after a long period of time, the tragic fact that he hadn't truly and earnestly repented. What really had happened was that the boy was as sorry as anybody ever could be. He said to me, "I wouldn't have taken it if I had known it was your car." I had never seen him before. But the worst thing about it for him was that he got caught. If he had only got through with that car and got rid of it, and I hadn't been hurt, and nobody else had been hurt much, then all would have been wonderful.

Penitence is always to be proved by its works. There is a verse in the Bible that says bring forth works "meet for repentance." And repentance, if it's the real thing, has to be followed by an absolute willingness to do anything—*anything*—to get right. I found that to any proposal I made to this boy there was always a counterproposal. If we would do thus and so, he would do thus and so. What can I get out of it if I do this? Or if I do the other thing, does that mean I can get free?

If a person has a real sense of guilt, and wants redemption, he must want it bad enough to quit doing wrong. Here's a good test. If you think you've repented about something that you've done, you can check yourself with this question: Have you quit?

For repentance is really being sorry enough to quit. The very word means to turn around and go the other way. And unless you do that, it's only words. That's why I like the words from the Communion—"Ye that do truly and earnestly repent." True repentance means you can't fool yourself. And it also means you can't fool God. If a thing is wrong, it's wrong against the nature of God; it's against the nature of the universe.

Something happens when you do wrong. Something happens to the moral order. If you throw a rock in a pool, the ripples are sure to go out to the shore. Or if a child lifts a spoonful of water from the ocean, every molecule in the ocean readjusts itself to that disturbance. The ocean's got a lot to do, because there are a lot of other disturbances, so it's constantly readjusting. I suppose everything in the physical world is like that. You lift up this book and disturb the universe! In the moral order everything gets disturbed by evil actions. Everything is affected in some small fashion; maybe the action's minute, infinitesimal, but it disturbs the universe. And it can't be pushed to one side; it can't be forgotten; it can only be forgiven. When we sin, we do something to God. We break the sense of fellowship; God does not break it, we break it. We cut the communication lines. Our prayers fail to rise, they fall to the ground, and nothing happens. We develop a hardness of heart and are not sensitive any more. A woman said to me one time, "I never cry now."

The next step from here is an attempt at rationalization. We want to justify what we do. We argue about it; and when we are told that what we have done is black, we try to make it into gray if we can't make it into white. The invitation insists, "Ye that do *truly* . . ." This means there isn't any fooling. It has to be the real thing. And then the word "earnestly" is added, and that means

17

we have to "sincerely desire." I think the word "earnestly" was put in there to say to us, "You have to press for it." We have to have the same intensity about this that we would have in other things we are pursuing with all our hearts. You know how intense we can be about something we're vitally interested in. What's the thing that is interesting you most right now? Think of *it*. There must be something you want desperately. Well then, we must repent with the same intensity that we show in other things we are interested in. We must sense the need for forgiveness, in that same intense way. We have to pursue it. There is urgency in it. "Ye that do *truly* and *earnestly* repent," the call insists. It means being sorry enough to quit.

Real repentance comes from within. It cannot be a surface experience. No one can bluff or side-step this demand. Here we meet God alone. I think there is much value in talking to a psychiatrist, or a counselor, or a minister, or a trusted friend. I think there is value in finding some other human being who will listen in an understanding manner. If you have nobody in all the world to whom you can talk, I think that's most unfortunate. There are people who have no one in whom to confide. If you're in that state, and there isn't any person to listen to you, there is still another way open; for God himself can and will hear the plaintive cry of the lonely soul. That's why I think there is so much of redemption in true communion. Many people pray sincerely for the first time as they commune. I won't know how you approach Communion, but for me, I try to be quiet. I certainly think people ought to have a chance to think and to have some moments alone.

A woman told me recently about her husband who was a member of another church. She said he goes to church about once a year. And when he comes home, he says, "Well, I confessed."

She said, "I used to ask him *what* he confessed." He'd say, "Just the same thing I confessed last year." And he'd get angry when she wanted to know just what he *did* confess. "Well," he said, "just the same as I did last year."

Can we expect repentance to work a miracle when we do the same thing over and over? How can we truly and earnestly repent in that fashion? How can one do a thing over and over and find any place for real repentance in that process? So penitence presupposes not only sorrow—sorrow that will make us quit our sinful practice; it also means we won't want to sin again. Even when we are forgiven, the hurt is still there. If it has been true repentance, we will not want to travel that road again because it isn't an easy road.

Some time ago I heard the story of a prisoner who had an amazing experience of redemption right in his prison cell. He had been filled with resentment and hatred and finally got to the place where he wanted to get even with the world. He was brought into his cell tied up, and when they released him, he fell unconscious on the brick floor. And this is what he said: "I have no knowledge of ever praying, or anything else. All I know is that when I regained consciousness, I was in the arms of God. I got up off that floor and resolved never again to do anything consciously against the will of God." He didn't even pray for forgiveness— forgiveness just rolled down upon him. I can't explain that, but I can understand this: just as soon as he got a chance, he asked to see the chaplain and said, "I don't want to get out. I want to spend the rest of my life trying to tell these other fellows how wonderful it is to be redeemed." He said, "If this is where God wants me, I'll stay right in this cell." There wasn't any more rebellion in his heart; there was nothing but utter love for mankind and for God.

*19*

And that's the real fruit of repentance. I would say that when a person gets to the place where he is willing to stay anywhere or do anything—pay any price—he's proved that he has produced "works meet for repentance."

So, "Ye that do truly and earnestly repent" is a beautiful part of the invitation to commune, and it's the *first station* on the Way of Wonder. There are a lot of other good stops, and they get more wonderful, but this one is inescapable. If you don't go through this one, you can't go on to the others. And the Way of Wonder will close. Instead of being a Way of Wonder it will be just a way of desolation, a dead-end street. There are some people I know who make too much of their sins; they dwell on them much too long. I think they doubt God. But God has promised that he will forgive, and when we have his promise, then all we need to do is to ask the sincere question, "Have I truly and earnestly repented?" And, having done that, we may trust in his forgiveness and start "walking in his holy ways."

# TWO

## *The Neighbor*

Y E THAT . . . are in love and charity with your neighbors. . . ." The first demand on the one who approaches the Communion seems reasonable—he must repent. No unrepentant person could hope to get much help. However, when we hear this second phrase, it seems an intrusion. Why should we have to be concerned with our neighbor? What does he have to do with our Communion?

Most of us can recall having had some very wonderful neighbors. Go back over your own experience and you will find that you have had more good neighbors than bad ones. I can recall only one or two who I thought were bad. That is why this phrase about neighbors seems almost an intrusion. It is somewhat like starting out on a road, a toll road, and the gates go down! And there's not just one gate, but many. Gate number one is the gate of *penitence*. If we pay the price we think all the gates should open and we ought to be able to move on, but—no! Our way is blocked, and we must face the question of our relation to our neighbors. We wish we could side-step this. We feel as though we should keep our Communion on a higher plane. It should be just between ourselves and God. But the "neighbor" will not disappear from our thoughts. He's as bothersome in our religious affairs as he is in our street. To ask a person to love his neighbor and to be charitable toward him is to risk a good deal. It's very hard. How can we concentrate on the Holy Communion if we have to be thinking of our neighbor and our relation to him? Why should we be bothered by thoughts about our neighbors when we are about to take the Communion? But it always happens! We start searching for God and we are asked about our attitude toward other people.

Who are these neighbors anyway? This question was asked a long time ago, and it was answered by the Master himself in the parable of the good Samaritan. The neighbor may be someone who lives a long way from you, or he may live next door. He is always a person who is in need and who needs us. And he becomes a neighbor because he is in need. If we tried to force him to love us, we would have a difficult task. We might not have much of a leverage upon him. But we're not asked to change him; we are only asked to have a good attitude toward him, no matter how stubborn or unreasonable he may be. And that we can do.

Our neighbor appears early in the invitation to Communion, simply because our outside relationships do have a way of intruding themselves into our prayers. We must face our neighbor first. Remember that verse—"If thou bring thy gift to the altar, and there rememberest that thy brother hath ought against thee; leave there thy gift . . . , and go thy way; first be reconciled to thy brother, and then come and offer thy gift." Now I think many would call that an unreasonable demand. "That would never work with my neighbor," we say. "He's unreasonable. I'm not going to be foolish. Anyhow, how can I be reconciled with someone when I've done him no wrong? Especially with a person who imagines that he's been mistreated?"

The answer to this is that no such demand is made upon us. Listen to it again—If on bringing your gift to the altar, you remember that your brother *hath ought against you*. . . Now if he really has nothing against you, and only imagines that he has, that's something else. If he's cooked up an idea—if he's a psychopathic enemy, if he's so utterly unreasonable that there isn't any basis for the thing he has imagined—certainly God doesn't ask us to change him, nor does God expect us to worry about him. If I were to try to win over every person who dislikes what I say, I'd surely be kept busy. But if he *has* something against me—ah! That's different! We have a chance to do something about that. What are you told to do? Well, leave your gifts at the altar and go and be reconciled. You must take care of that neighbor's just accusation before you start traveling this road, this Way of Wonder. The tollgate is down, the toll is demanded, and reconciliation is the price.

Now some will say, "Oh, that couldn't be. He would never forgive me," or "She would never do it." Of course, the only way we can know about that is to try. It's an amazing thing, though, that whenever we've made an honest effort, we're quite surprised to find that the other person is just as anxious as we are. Did you every try to get anything fixed up with somebody when you thought you couldn't possibly do it? And wasn't it the most rewarding experience? Suppose the person does have something against you and you know it, and you make the long trip, the difficult trip, toward reconciliation. You can almost depend upon this, that the other person is just as eager to get the matter fixed up as you. Sometimes the joy of reconciliation exceeds any

*23*

joy a human being can ever experience, especially when two people who have been estranged find out that both of them want the same thing, and that is to forgive and to be forgiven. I don't know anything that hurts more than to know you're estranged from somebody. It puts upon us a sense of strain, especially if it continues over a long period of time. When it's wiped away it all seems so foolish, and the joy that accompanies reconciliation is so satisfying that you wonder why you put it off so long.

It must be the same way with God. That's why the Bible says there's joy in heaven over one sinner who repents, more than over the ninety and nine who need no repentance. God longs to bring back the wayward sheep. He can never be satisfied while they are out on the distant hills, even if there are ninety and nine safely in the fold. I cannot think that God will ever quit trying to bring about a reconciliation as long as there is one left out. I don't know how long it will take him to bring us back. I suppose a thousand years mean nothing to God, because a day with the Lord is as a thousand years. Time, in this sense, has no meaning. Don't you suppose God will get us at last? There's no doubt about punishment for sin, but the Father's heart is always yearning to receive the penitent, and when we come back home, there is great joy, and everything is different.

If you are carrying on a continuous battle with someone and have secretly longed for reconciliation, why not try to get the trouble straightened out? If you fail, if it can't be done, God is not going to ask the unreasonable or the impossible. When a person has never made such an attempt, he has no idea what a wonderful experience forgiveness can be. Write that letter tonight. A word, a telephone call, or a friendly glance may be enough. Be willing to take that first step. That is the one, the first step, the hard one—and following it comes reconciliation.

We turn now to three or four things that we can gather out of this—the conclusions we come to about our attitude toward our neighbor. We're not told in detail what the love of our neighbor really means, although the Bible makes great use of this word "love." Five times in the Bible the sentence "Love thy neighbor" appears in this exact form, and in several other instances it is implied. We're told: "Thou shalt love the Lord thy God with all thy heart, and with all thy soul, and with all thy mind. This is the first and great commandment. And the second is like unto it [or of just about the same quality], Thou shalt love thy neighbour as thyself." It would be easy to get into a rhapsody about the meaning of love. But we're not talking about the kind of love that would make us overlook reality. I think the best description of it is the Bible's own command— Love your neighbor as yourself. Sometimes you don't love yourself very much. That is, you've had times when you knew you were wrong and when you almost hated yourself. You say, "Why did I do such a thing?" I don't believe anybody can love his neighbor intelligently and honestly and in a Christlike way without taking into account the limitations that we all have of our own. We can't love ourselves when we are sinful, and we can't condone evil in a neighbor. I think it's an attitude. It's an outgoing from the heart. It's a spirit of willingness to forgive. It's an attempt to understand.

I like this phrase from the invitation—I think it's added there to give a little more light. It says you must be in "love *and charity* with your neighbors." I think I can understand charity better; that is, I know how to be charitable. And while the word "charity" is translated "love," it does have a little different flavor. We understand charity because we see through Christian eyes what it means to be charitable. It's giving the other person the benefit of the doubt—not looking for every little thing to pick apart and find fault with, but trying to see how many things we can appreciate rather than depreciate. It's a tendency to put the best kind of interpretation, the best possible construction, on the other person's actions. It's the effort to really see the total person rather than just his mean streaks. In charity we try to see why people are as they are—to understand what produced them and out of what kind of situation they came. We try to remember the kind of struggle they have endured and the heartaches they have had. All these are involved in this matter of love and charity.

These are the things about the neighbor that seem to me to be true. First, a neighbor is a means of grace for us. That is, he's put in our pathway in order to do something *for* us. We may be able to do something for him, but he is doing something for us. He blocks our prayers. He stands at the altar rail right in front of us, and until we get him out of the way we can't commune. This neighbor of ours becomes a means of defeat, or a means of grace. Stanley Jones used to say, "My critics are the unpaid watchmen of my soul." That was quite a thing to say. It's hard to believe, but it is really true that the people who have been severe and maybe unreasonable in their criticism have called attention to something in us that is wrong, at least in a measure. And lo! this critic turns out to be working for us, and he does it all without pay. Most of us would take him off the payroll if there was one. Most of us think we could do without our critics. We think one or two of them would be enough, but the critic, or the neighbor—

the person who is difficult, the person who is hard to get along with—does become a means of grace.

That leads me to the second step—the neighbor becomes a test of our sincerity. If our Christian communion could be between us and God alone, wouldn't it be better? If it could be something that we could carry on in private! If only our religion had nothing to do with life! It is that way in many parts of the world. I was amazed at what I saw in some of the temples of the East. I remember one in Benares, India. I went only as far as the door. None of us wanted to go in. The scenes depicted within were vile. I saw a nice class of children out under the shade of a tree, just beyond this heathen temple. A Buddhist priest was teaching religion to them. When I tried to get some explanation of it, about all I could learn was that such things had nothing to do with the spiritual life. That is, life and religion were divorced. What you believe and the way you tried to approach God were unrelated to the way you acted. This temple was the earthly expression of the evil in us. There was another temple, a spiritual one. The one of this earth was there to show you just how bad you could be, and the spiritual one to point out how good! I could never get that point of view! It is not the view of the New Testament. In the teaching of Jesus our religion and our life are very closely related. It's God and man. It's man and his neighbor. Our business is related to our worship, and you just can't separate them.

I remember preaching a sermon once on "The Sanctuary and the Street." I tell you, you have to have a street in order to have a sanctuary. In other words, you have to help people. I tried to teach my grandson this little couplet:

Here's the church and here's the steeple.
Open the door and there's the people.

He got his hands put together the wrong way and he said: "Here's the church and here's the steeple. Open the door and . . . ," he added with surprise, "there aren't any people." That's often the trouble. A church without people isn't a church. It is only a building. A religion that has no relation to other people isn't much of a religion. This is the way to test religion—if it doesn't relate itself to people and their problems, it isn't religion in the real sense.

Furthermore, a neighbor is a challenge to our concern. Some years ago I served on a missionary committee. Applicants were being selected for the foreign field. We had one girl who was very anxious to go, and her application was in order. She had a good scholastic record. She was in good health. She seemed to have a great desire to serve, but as we sought to find out more and more about her real reasons for wanting to go, she said, "I always thought it would be wonderful to help people." We asked her more about the country she had chosen, but she seemed to know nothing about it. She had read nothing. She just thought there were people there who were in great need. We asked her where she lived and what she thought about people of other races in her own town. She didn't know whether there were any there or not, for she had never known one of them. She had never talked with anyone of another race. She had known a girl in her college who knew a colored girl very well, but she didn't know the colored girl!

I remember a young man who said to our committee that he wanted to be of help to "migrant workers." He had read *Grapes of Wrath.* He pictured such people as needing his help. We asked him if had ever seen a migrant worker. He hadn't. He wouldn't have had to go very far. They were just across the lake from his home! They were the people who gathered the fruit or who worked in the nearby wheat fields. After all, they're people. You can't be interested in Indians or Chinese in the Far East and fail to be interested in Indians and Chinese on your street. You can't be interested in human beings on the other side of the world and have no interest in people who live in the next apartment. It's so strange that we always want to save people who live far from us.

This, then, is the test we apply to ourselves as we come to the Lord's table. Are we in love and charity with our neighbors? I know they are bothersome and may interfere with our Communion, but these neighbors walk right up to the altar rail with us and challenge our concern. Do we really care about them?

The neighbor has this last and final function in our Communion. He becomes a "passport." If we have the right attitude toward our neighbor, he will pay the fare. The tollgate will go up and we will start on our way of Communion. Wonderful that a neighbor can do all that for us, wonderful that just because we get in the right relationship the gate opens, but it really does, and you know it does. Haven't you ever had that happen? Sometimes these neighbors are, as we have said, a long way apart. Sometimes they're close. Sometimes they're right in the family. It's hard to think of a neighbor as being a person who is related to us, such as a husband or a wife, or one of the children, or some other member of the family, but it means the same thing.

I clearly recall two men who were brothers and who lived as

29

neighbors. One—we'll call him Will, and the other one Charlie. They had their homes in the country. I went to preach in that community and I couldn't accomplish anything at all. When I'd ask people what was the matter—that I thought there was something wrong here that I couldn't figure out—they would look puzzled and say, "No, there isn't anything that we know of." I asked the minister and he didn't know. Nobody knew anything. I think they did not want to have an old wound opened up. It turned out that these two brothers had actually split that church. One of them had a faction around him, and the other had one around him, and they weren't speaking. They carried on this feud until finally the thing was organized. They even got so that they sat in different parts of the church. Their wives took up the cause. You see, the wives of these two brothers indoctrinated their children, and then their cousins, and on through the family. They didn't know for sure what it was all about, but they were just as bitter as the principals. It was as bad as the Martins and the Coys—a feud going on right in this little Methodist church. I said, "I don't think anything good will happen in this church as long as this thing continues."

I insisted that we have it out. I was young then, inexperienced and foolhardy, and I insisted that unless we got them together I was going to leave. I suppose if they had known just how green I was, they might have let me go, but they didn't know what I intended doing. I asked them to come for a visit. When they got together, I sat in the room with them. They just sat there and glowered at each other. The wives sat back of them a little way, and they were even worse. I thought they must have had axes. They were just so angered. And then, finally, after we talked around and around and it just seemed like all accusation—nobody confessing anything, nobody admitting anything—finally I did the thing I've done so many times when I didn't know what else to do. I said, "Let us unite in prayer."

I asked them to kneel. Mind you, these people were workers in the church. One of them was superintendent of the Sunday school, and the other one was teaching a class. So I called on the superintendent to lead us in prayer. Well, he began by praying for China or some such distant place. I remember he prayed for a lot of things, but none of them had anything to do with that little church, and nothing to do with his brother or the divided church. And yet it's hard to talk to God without getting into trouble—or out of it. I don't know whether he squinted out of the corner of his eye or not, but something must have mellowed him because there was a little break in his voice. And then I called on the other one. And in the midst of it—I can't tell yet, I don't remember just what happened—but in the midst of it there was a little tone of confession, a little plea to God for forgiveness. It wasn't much, but it was enough, and I heard sobbing. I give you my word, before they got through that prayer meeting that night in that little room, they were hugging each other, and they were all fixing things up. Such happiness I have seldom witnessed!

I went back there some months later. It was election time, and I saw a car going by on the way to election, and I asked who it was. It was Charlie and Will and the children all crowded in the car. They couldn't be separated even when they went into town. They had found reconciliation—the sweetest thing they had ever experienced in their lives.

Well, it's that way. When you're estranged, you can't be happy. When you break fellowship within the Christian faith, you break with God. If we are truly "in love and charity with our neighbors" the tollgate goes up and we start on our Way of Wonder. Thank God for our neighbors! Who'd want to live in a world without them! They may be in the next apartment, or in a country on the other side of the globe. The land between China and America joins in the center of the earth. There must be a spot in the middle of the earth where *all* lands come together. I know that in the heart of God there's a place that unites us all because we're all members of his family. Thank God for the neighbor.

# THREE

&#x2299;

## *The Great Intention*

A ND NOW we come to the theme "The Great Intention." To understand it we have to get at the word "intention." "... And *intend* to lead a new life" is the phrase in the invitation.

I remember, and this was a long time ago, a boy and a girl who had a date or two. The father of the girl said to the boy after the second date, "We would like to know what your intentions are." The boy proceeded to get out of there as fast as he could because he didn't have any intentions. He thought that the father intended marriage, and the boy only wanted a date. From that time on, the word "intention" has taken on other shades of meaning. One of those strangely different meanings is brought out in the question, "Do you intend to lead a new life?"

Suppose we put the question in a little different way—"What's your design?" Sometimes the word *intention* means *plan*. "What are your plans?" Sometimes the word takes on the meaning of *purpose*. "What's your purpose?" Intention is always related, in a sense, to the future. It doesn't present a bill for the past as does the word "repentance." It's a kind of blueprint. That's why intention is so important in our Christian faith.

I grew up in Dallas, Iowa—a town so little that we had no railroad. It was fourteen miles to the nearest railroad, and I had never seen a train until I was twelve years old, when we made a trip to the county seat and we went to see the train come in. I got excited when I saw it coming. That little pencil of light kept getting larger and larger and larger. I suppose it wasn't a very powerful light in front of that little engine, but it looked like some great eye to me. The train went straight through that town and never stopped. It threw cinders in my eyes, but I just threw my hat up in the air and yelled with excitement.

Then I remember the day that some surveyors came through *our* little town and set out stakes. On pieces of lath they wrote in blue chalk some hieroglyphics that I couldn't understand. They said, "Do you know what? They intend to build a railroad." I've heard some things since then, but I don't think anything could stir my mind as much as that phrase, "They *intend* to build a railroad through Dallas." That word, at that moment, had a great meaning. I didn't know until later that some college engineering students used to survey across the countryside for practice—and a good dinner. When they had run their line across some farmer's barnyard, he'd give them a good dinner to set the stakes over on the other side of the place. But when I did find out, the word "intention" didn't suffer. Intentions are powerful.

I suppose you've heard the expression "The way to hell is paved with good intentions." Old Dr. Johnson—you remember the one Boswell wrote about—had something to say about that. He said, and I think he was right, that the way to hell is paved with *bad* intentions. Good intentions put us on the road to heaven. Actually, you are the intentions of yesterday. So am I. We may not like to admit it, but we are what we wanted to be.

I won't press the point. It gets uncomfortable. We like to blame our condition today on a thousand things, but we are pretty much what we planned to be. We are the result of our yesterdays. If we've made a mess of things, we can blame it on many things, but part of the blame can be placed on our intents and purposes.

My grandson used to ask when tomorrow would come. I would say to him, "Well, tomorrow, you know, is in the morning." He'd always be right there in the morning to know, "Is this tomorrow?" Finally I thought I'd be clever and I said to him, "Well, now, you see today is yesterday's tomorrow." He looked a little mystified and I began to feel the same way. What I was trying to tell him was that there is always a world in the making. Some of it seems to be here, and some of it is reaching out like a bridge to the other shore. I can imagine that some of our great bridges seemed to reach out toward the ends of the earth. So our dreams and our intentions reach—reach—reach. Finally the blueprint, the design, of our intention becomes the real structure. The reaching is over, and the other shore is before us.

When I give the invitation to commune, I come to these words, "Ye that do truly and earnestly repent . . . and intend to lead a new life." Not every person in the congregation, I suppose, follows closely and says to himself, "Now, let's see, what do I really intend to do?" Some people might have to answer that question in strange ways, "I intend to get out of here as quickly as I can," or "Let's get it over with." And some people would come up with a list of things they intend to do—later. But we cannot get much help out of the Communion without having some real intentions.

I remember a boy who came to me years ago. His mother

wanted me to talk to him. She said, "I don't know what's the matter with this boy. I can't get anything out of him. He just seems to have no ambition." So I agreed to talk to him. I said, "John, what do you like to do?" I thought I'd better put him at ease, so I tried again, "John, just relax and tell me honestly what is the thing you really want to do?" He thought a bit and he said, "Well, eat."

I could understand that, but I said, "Now beyond eating, what do you really want to do, John?" He took a little longer that time but finally he said, "Well, sleep." I said, "Now let's go beyond eating and sleeping. What do you like to do? What do you really want to do above everything else?" That seemed to stir him, and he said, with a good deal of enthusiasm, "Read the funnies."

I spent about twenty minutes with that fellow and I never got him beyond the funny page. He couldn't think of a single thing on earth that he really wanted to do beyond that: eat, sleep, and read the funnies. I had to hand him back to his mother and I felt almost as though she really ought to turn him in on a new model. I hope that somebody finally found a way to stimulate that fellow. I don't know what you can do with a person like that. His intentions were not very high. I doubt if you could call them intentions.

What do you intend? I intend to lead a new life, so help me God. That's the attitude we ought to have in Communion. God planned our life for more than eating, sleeping, reading the funnies.

Why, then, are you here? Some of you because friends brought you, or you had a little spare time. Some because of curiosity, perhaps. For the most part we are seeking something. What is it?

One of the things we want is fellowship. We want to meet somebody. We want to see somebody. We want to be with people who believe as we do. Outside the walls of the church life is so different, so impersonal. Here we are a part of a worshiping congregation and we feel that we count for something in the fellowship.

That's not all, of course; we want to have status too. We want to be, as well as to belong. We want to know that we aren't just one more unknown person hurrying along the street. We are God's children, and we aren't happy until we are recognized as belonging to him.

Some of us want a better faith, a clearer understanding. Things sometimes get distorted. We don't seem to see clearly. I recall having trouble making color pictures. They kept coming back from the processing laboratory with the same kind of streak on them. I reported it. I got a new roll of film because I complained about that fuzzy streak. I finally found out what it was. Since the camera was a little one, I had been sticking my finger in front of the lens and taking pictures of the end of my finger. Perhaps life has been distorted for you. What you are doing may be resulting in poor pictures of your life as it should be lived. What is your intention? What are you going to do about the distortions in your faith?

Intentions are often born out of those moments when we begin to realize that something is wrong. Our vague apprehensions, our peculiar emotions, our distorted ideas, lead to a general dissatisfaction with ourselves. After that comes the desire to lead a new life, and this is the *great intention*. All the while that you are intending to lead the new life, God is intending to reach you.

That's the wonder of it—a two-way street to the love of God. No sooner do you start than you realize that God has been coming to meet you. Think again of the bridge. While you are building from your end of the bridge, God is building from his.

Just what does God intend for us? That's really worth a series of sermons. He seems to intend a beautiful world, the way he has made it. He's trying to do something different, apparently, because he never makes two people alike, nor two blades of grass alike, nor two snowflakes, nor two grains of sand. We parents may try to make our youngsters over to be like us. We are prone to look for a duplicate of the old pattern. We feel flattered when someone says, "Just like his dad." But that is not so good. What if the world were full of duplicates? We hide carbons in files and let the letter go on its way. Why do parents want their children to be exactly like themselves? God's great intention isn't that we become just like our parents. He intended something better than they were—than we are.

An inventor who is of some importance told me that he never stops just because he's done with a job. "As soon as I get a machine off the drawing boards, before ever a piece of the machine is cast, I try to design a machine to beat it. If I don't do that, my competitor will." I think God is trying to do something like that. His intention must be to match his physical world with something more adequate in the moral and spiritual realm. God is trying to make your life more Christlike. God is trying to lure you into the higher realm of selfless living.

Suppose it turns out that God is trying to use you to rid the world of some of its jealousy, and hatred, and meanness? Suppose he is trying to start with you—with me? Perhaps he's trying to get us to be unselfish or to fill our empty hearts with his love.

You may be sure that he is doing everything he can with the kind of product he has to work with.

Even an animal will respond to love. The response may be poor, but most of the time he'll return your love. I visited a home once in a community where I had a preaching engagement. When I stepped into the house, a dog jumped toward the door where I stood. The preacher who was my host went to the dog and started talking to him. In a little while he persuaded the dog that I wasn't worth bristling up about. He gave that dog to understand that I was the preacher of the evening and that I wasn't to be chewed up. Before long the dog came and looked up at me. All at once I couldn't read my notes. He had reached over and nuzzled up against me. I patted his head and that dog didn't stop trucking around me all that evening. Every time I tried to move, the dog was there. How quickly he had responded! Perhaps, in a remote way, even plants and trees and flowers respond. We talk about those "green thumbs." Sometimes I wonder.

How do we respond to God? Suppose that God is trying to bring something out of us and doesn't get much response. Suppose we complain constantly about our lot, or bristle at fancied troubles. Yet God keeps trying to grow something better. He wants us to develop into the children of God that we know we ought to be.

If you intend to lead the new life, God intends for you to have it. If it is your intention to follow the commandments of God and lead a different life, God intends to help you win that battle. He intends nothing less than perfection, nothing less than fulfillment of what you may really become.

Think of the patience of God, of how long he works to bring us nearer perfection! He started with our great, great-grandparents. Some of mine were in England, some in Ireland, and some came to this country. At a given time and place—in Ohio, or Pennsylvania, or Canada, or Kentucky—your grandparents rejoiced in the birth of a child—your father—your mother. Your parents rejoiced in your birth. Possibly long before that time the great intention of God began for you. He "meant for you to be," as a song puts it. God intended not only to bring you into being, but to work with you. His intention was never less than perfection. He has a long job ahead with me, but he is still at work.

There was only one in whom God had that perfection he sought for in the children of men. Even when the hatred of man put Christ up on a cross, God was there. People who stood around during those awful moments thought it thundered. Some didn't know what to make of it when the temple veil was rent in twain, but God was there through it all. No wonder the crowd felt so strange when Jesus talked to God and called him "Father." God intended Christ. I think he intends us to be as near to that likeness of divine love as he can get us to be.

The great intention results in a meeting of the desire of our hearts with the will of God. It comes from two directions. There is the intention of God to call us into being and toward perfection. There is the intention of our own heart to be conformed to God's will. That produces what we call the great intention. There is a verse in the book of Jeremiah which reads: "Until he [has] performed the intents of his heart. . . ." This reveals the persistence of God's intention toward us. How long? Until his intention is fulfilled. How long? Until we surrender. How long? Until this world comes to a saving knowledge of him. How long? Until the kingdoms of this world become the kingdoms of our Lord and of his Christ! That's the intention of God. No wonder we can call it the great intention.

# FOUR

## *Walking in His Ways*

I INVITE you now to think of the phrase "walking in his ways." The whole quotation goes like this: "and walking from henceforth in his holy ways." Its meaning is clear in the invitation. We have been told to repent, but now we have come to the place where we must do something more than repent. At this point we must begin to *do* something. If you feel that you are "in love and charity with your neighbors" and you have the intention to lead a new life with the help of God, you must now start walking in his ways—you must begin doing something about it. This demands action and moves us toward some results. It suggests something we can do.

The word "ways" in the Bible is used over and over. Take a concordance and look down the list. The word, with its synonyms, appears hundreds of times. Often the word has reference to "paths"—"the paths of the Lord" or "the ways of the Lord." One of the early uses of the word is in Second Samuel, "The *way* of the Lord is perfect." You will recall how the first psalm ends with the statement, "The way of the ungodly shall perish." I remember hearing a sermon by the pastor of our church in my boyhood. He quoted this verse, "A highway shall be there, and a way, and it shall be called The way of holiness." The preacher believed in a "second blessing." Everybody is on the highway, he said, but only a few get on this holy way. This was a way for the special—for the few.

There is a sense in which that is true. When the children of Israel were moving to the Promised Land, they didn't have much of a trip so far as miles are concerned, but they wandered around, retracing their steps, milling around without making progress. You can make the same trip now in about half an hour by plane. By automobile it would be an easy trip if it were not for having to cross disputed boundaries. But the trip was a *way*. A pillar of cloud led the people by day, and a pillar of fire by night. Over and over again they referred to the "way" the Lord was leading them. And he would have led them straight through if they had been obedient, but they wouldn't take that road.

One of the first things you run into in the New Testament is the story of John the Baptist. "Prepare ye the way of the Lord" was his message. When you hear a choir sing it, it is a thrilling challenge. His commission is ours too. Being a Christian is not just believing something, or holding to an ideal, but it's a call to clear the track and prepare the way as though the Lord could get to a place only when we make it possible. It suggests that we can even help God accomplish his purpose by "preparing a way." John the Baptist believed this and talked it.

Do you remember, in the story of the birth of Jesus, that the wise men from the East "went home by another way"? I'd like to think that they were different men after they saw the Christ Child. It is true that people who have ever been to that cradle go home by a different road. That is one of the uses of this word "way." Of course, you also find the use of such expressions after Jesus' death and resurrection. You remember he was walking along on the Emmaus road. The disciples were worried and they said, "We thought it was Christ who was to deliver us, and now he's dead." The scripture says they walked and talked with Jesus "on the way." What a way that one was— a lonely, discouraged way! They walked along with him, unaware of his presence, and thought everything had collapsed. They felt as we do when we see all our schemes fail and when life tumbles in. But Christ was there, really there beside them, and they didn't realize it. The only thing they were sure of was that their hearts burned within them. The burning heart is still one of the best evidences that we are on his way.

Some time ago I met with a group of ministers, four hundred of them, in the mountains of Pennsylvania. These busy ministers were from many different types of communities. But there we were singing together and praying together, and an amazing thing happened: we began to feel a sense of oneness, with burning hearts. You know, the Master said, "Where two or three are gathered together in my name, there am I." And it is true! If you're of one mind and one spirit, and are in one place, you are fulfilling the conditions that brought about that first Pentecost. The group of ministers I was with had the same experience again that afternoon. It was Pentecost for us. As I left the hall to get in the car and start for the plane a hundred miles away, I could still hear them singing, and I realized all over again the wonder of the experience of Pentecost. One of the last things I had been trying to tell these ministers was that, far beyond any theology or any schemes we might devise, the burning heart—the feeling that you care—is most important. Every time anyone sins

WALKING IN HIS WAYS

it affects all of us. The hurt of the world descends on all of us;
it causes us to have a "burning heart" indeed. Many of you have
experienced it. It's as if there was a hurt, like a broken heart.
When your heart is aching and you feel you're identified with
the hurts of other people, you're getting more like Christ, because he carried our sins in his own body. He was touched with
the feelings of our infirmities. He traveled that road; it was a holy
way. We may have to walk that kind of way too. All these
"ways" are like paths. Walking in his holy ways means walking
in his holy paths.

But now there is another whole group of ways. They are
"ways" of doing things. It's as though we referred to Christ's way
of life. If we were talking about our ways we might speak of
our "philosophy of life." We all have one, and we usually live
according to it. You say, "Not me—I don't care what happens."
Very well, that's a philosophy—the philosophy of "I don't care."

As a boy I used to go to the drugstore, where there was a
marvelous soda fountain with its marble counter and a long
list of flavors. The clerk would pull one of those round handles
and the thing would fill a glass. In those days a soda didn't have
ice cream in it, just soda and flavoring, but there was vanilla,
chocolate, strawberry, and sarsaparilla, and then over at the end
there was one called "Don't Care." When they asked a country
boy who was a little fussed anyway what he wanted, he was
likely to say, "I don't care," so they had that one labeled "Don't
Care." It really was made up of a combination of all the other
flavors, so they would just fizz one out of that for him. Well, in
some such fashion we have a philosophy of "I Don't Care," but
it's real nevertheless. For some people, it would mean "I'm
looking out for No. 1." This is my interest—I'm thinking of me,

*45*

me, mine, mine. "I can't get this—I will get that." Well, that's a philosophy. Fortunately, there are many other people who are living unselfishly. Their philosophy causes them to do whatever they can to lift the load for others, and they follow that philosophy.

In contrast to this, the *way* that I am talking about—this holy *way*—is trying to follow Christ's way of living. It is of God. "As for God, his way is perfect." "Strait is the gate, and narrow is the way," Jesus said. This does not necessarily mean a narrow road. Narrow is the procedure of living; strait is the gate and narrow is this holy way of life.

The first Christians didn't have a name. People didn't know what to call them, so they just referred to them as "followers of the way." You will find the phrase in some of the ancient documents. What kind of way? Oh, the way to live! They had found a way to live. They had found out that there was something to live for. They were now out beyond themselves—followers of the way.

We note now a third definition. Sometimes you run into this expression: "The way of all the earth." So this way is not only a pathway of life, but sometimes the way seems to be referring to *death*. "The way of all flesh"—most of us use that expression. "I guess it's gone the way of all the earth" means it's gone down the drain or up in smoke, or the plan has fizzled, disintegrated. For many people life is like that. They feel it's all washed up. A young man said to me when I talked to him in jail, "Well, it's no use any more; I'm through." "Oh," I said, "there'll come a day when you'll hardly be able to remember this if you start from here and begin to live right." "No," he said, "I don't think so. I think it's all over." It wasn't all over, of course, but that's a "way," and one which is in direct contrast to God's holy ways, for they are never finished. They're never over. They're never down the drain or up in smoke. Contrast, if you will, the way of all the earth with the way of God which is *never* through. The *way* of God is forever!

"Walking henceforth in his holy ways." I like that! We can walk—I doubt if we can "ride" although that would be the first thing we would want to do. A student minister was talking to me once about a quick way to have Communion. "We can serve the whole business in ten minutes," he said. "Why don't you make it five?" I asked. It takes time to commune. We have to walk. It is nice to get in a car and cover a lot of miles, but there are some things you will never see unless you walk. At Niagara I was told, "If you really want to see the falls you'll have to get out." I said, "Oh, I'll just sit here." "No," the man said, "you get out." I said, "I can see them." "No," he said, "you can't really." Finally I got out and we walked through the mist. It was muddy, but we finally came to a platform out where we had a grand view of the Horseshoe Falls as well as the American Falls.

I'm not much of a walker; I don't like it, but I found out that when it comes to seeing spiritual things you have to walk. You must "walk in his holy ways." It doesn't say you are to run either. Many want to run and get it over with. They go to church in a hurry. They get it over in the morning. They say their prayers and they say them so fast! "Give me this." "Give me that." "Give me the other." They can repeat all those phrases that are supposed to interest God, but do we really suppose that God is interested in any of them? There's too much speed in running. Oh, there are admonitions in the Bible about running. Paul used them; he said, for instance, "Run with patience the race . . ."

47

I don't know just how you do that. It's hard to be patient when you're on a dead run, but anyway it's Paul's figure of speech. But Paul wasn't talking about the holy ways of God. He knew, as anybody else knows who has ever experienced the deep things of God, that there are things which will never be revealed on the run. It takes time to be holy. It takes time to become quiet. This Way of Wonder is never open to us unless we have allowed enough time. But, neither are we supposed to crawl. Some people feel like crawling. Sometimes the sense of our sin, or the sense of being no good at all, or of making such a failure, makes us feel that we'd like to crawl; but God has never asked for that. We are told to *walk*—walk in his holy way.

There's one more word in this phrase and I think it's as interesting as any—"walking from *henceforth* in his holy ways." The word "hence," so far as I know, means to go *out* of this place or *from* this place. We say, "Get thee hence," and we mean—get out! And when we say "henceforth," we mean go forward, since "forth" means "forward." We are supposed to move, to get out and go—*now,* right now! We want to start—tomorrow? You remember that Augustine was feeling penitent about his sin—and he surely had sinned enough to make him feel that way—and he prayed, "O God, make me clean . . . but not yet." And if you think he was a strange one, check yourself. We all want to be clean, we want to be good, we want to quit this bad habit. We're not going to talk about people anymore. We're not going to be jealous. We're not going to say unkind things. We will be more like Christ. "O God, make me clean . . . but not yet."

I remember a certain man in Chicago. He was running a tavern and he got so disturbed about it that he came to see me. His wife wanted him to get rid of the tavern, and he decided to sell

48

it. "I don't like to sell liquor," he said. "I tell you, I don't like it." And I said, "I don't think you could like it, for it will finally turn on you and it will hurt you. So, I don't blame you. I'd get out of it too." And he said, "That's just what I say, and I'm going to quit. I tell you what I think. I'm just going to keep operating the tavern long enough so I can get some money ahead—just so we can get along, you know. I think I can make enough out of it so we won't have to worry. I'm going to get rid of it then, but not yet."

Some years ago a man came to my front door when I was living in Rockford, Illinois—a man I used to go to prep school with. He had driven a hundred miles and he wanted me to speak at his club. He had driven all this way to ask me if I would do it. I said, "Well, I'd do it for you. Sit down," and we began to talk about old times. I asked, "How are you doing?" He said, "Oh, I'm all right." But there was something about him that I couldn't figure out. Calling him by the familiar name that I knew in school, I asked, "What's wrong? What's the matter?" "Well," he said, "you're a preacher. You know, I hated to come here to see you. I really had a hard time making myself come." "What in the world is wrong with that?" I wanted to know. "Well, I don't know," he answered. "I guess it's just that I'm wondering what you'd think of me." I said, "I think a lot of you." "But what about my business?" he asked.

And then he began a long story. His uncle had a tavern. It was a notorious place and under suspicion, when suddenly his uncle died. The old fellow had willed this evil institution to my friend. He asked, "Do you remember, Goff, that I used to think I was going into the ministry?" I said, "Yes, I certainly do; I remember that." "Well, I had that notion until then, and then this

49

thing was right in front of me. And you know what I did? I decided that I'd take it and I'd keep it long enough to get enough money so that I could go to school again." He fully intended to go through the seminary, but he had taken hold of something he couldn't turn loose. "Now," he said, "I'm tied to it. The thing's losing money. I've been in a lot of trouble and I can't get out."

His eyes dropped and he could hardly look at me. Finally he said, "But I'm going to do it." I said, "Well listen, fellow, why don't we do it now? Just let it go. Nothing in this world is so important as for you to get straightened out." But I got nowhere at all. He went out and got in his car. He's still at the tavern, tied to this evil thing, having compromised with something lower. He had a chance to start right then, but he found it was mighty hard to do. And when we start on this "way," we'd better be sure we mean "from now on."

Isn't it wonderful to know that God takes our sins and puts them behind his back and remembers them no more against us forever! Forever! That's a great word. What if we had to go back and relive our sins and have them brought back after forgiveness? What if there wasn't any way by which you could clean the slate, no real redemption, and the things were all piled up and had to be met? What if there was no grace of God? What if we could never come to an altar or find forgiveness? No wonder there have been so many people in this world who, weighted with such burdens, have become despondent. That's why we call the gospel the good news. That's why this way means so much to us.

There was a man sitting in the back of a chapel one morning who had just followed the crowd. He didn't know anything about the church. He heard the music. He heard the preacher. But

50

nothing was happening; he was just sitting there. He told me afterwards, "All of a sudden things began to flash." And there he was alone with God in the back of a chapel. He walked out of the chapel that day a different man. He had met God there all alone. You see, it's just like that when you start walking in "his holy ways."

# FIVE

# Draw Near with Faith

Assuming that you do truly and earnestly repent and are in love and charity with your neighbors, that you do intend to lead a new life, and that you do walk in his holy ways, then comes this suggestion, alive with meaning, "Draw near with faith."

Many people are old enough to remember when the leader used to "give out scripture passages" in the young people's meeting. He would give the passages, and then various ones would volunteer to take them. After searching through the Bible, they would stand up and read them. It was like feeding the verses *in* and then reversing the machine and grinding them *out.*

Well, I'm going to revert to a little of that and give you some passages, because that's the best way I know to set before you this matter of drawing near with faith. The first scripture is from the sixth chapter of John. "No man can come to me, except the Father which hath sent me draw him: and I will raise him up at the last day." The emphasis that we first make is that there is no drawing near to God unless he begins the process. It's a kind of magnetism, if you want to put it that way. The eternal God moves toward the lonely individual heart. So God calls us, God draws us, and that's *first*.

In John 12:32 you read these wonderful words: "And I, if I be lifted up from the earth, will draw all men unto me." Here we have the definite teaching that there's a magnetism about the cross, for Christ is speaking here of the cross. Who would ever suppose that the cross would have such a pull upon the human soul? It is the last thing in the world we'd ever expect to draw people. It's a repellent thing. But Jesus said, "I will draw all men unto me if I am lifted up," and he meant, "if I am lifted up on a cross."

How true! For right now, all over the world, wistful, longing, lonesome souls look at that figure and are drawn to it by some mysterious force. You can't keep your eyes off it. "And they that passed by reviled him, wagging their heads," but the world ever since has turned to take another look. A cross may be beautiful as an ornament, but this cross with Christ on it—well, that's something different. These other crosses are only symbolic, but it's never until you see Christ that you feel drawn toward the cross.

On a foggy night some years ago, a big crowd gathered on Madison Street in Chicago. The people were looking up at the cross on top of our downtown church, and the police couldn't get them out of the street. Finally the police had somebody go up and see, because everyone was saying that there was a man up there. Someone said, "I think he's going to commit suicide." Others said, "It's just a religious fanatic; he's trying to get up on the cross." The police actually had to send somebody up there in the dark to climb those ladders. A careful check was made, but there wasn't anybody on the cross. The fog was swirling around in such a way that it looked like somebody. And this went on there for two hours until the rain finally dispersed the crowd. I have thought of that experience many times. There are crosses all over the world, and nobody pays much attention to them until they think there's a man on the cross. What if they thought it was the Son of God!

We turn to another scripture passage in the book of Hebrews. Here we find this wonderful suggestion in the tenth chapter: "Let us draw near with a true heart in full assurance of faith, having our hearts sprinkled from an evil conscience, and our bodies washed with pure water." This is the direct source of the invitation to commune. The composer of that invitation went right straight to this passage, because this is it: "Let us draw near with a true heart in full assurance of faith." Just another way of saying, "Let us draw near with faith." The writer of the book of Hebrews, of course, is interested not only in "drawing near," he suggests some of the prerequisites—"our hearts sprinkled from an evil conscience." What he means is that there must be a cleansing —a washing—a preparation.

I remember holding a very large Communion service once, and the ministers who were going to help had come from a distance. We were to meet in the corridor outside the sanctuary. I surprised them by having a basin, a towel, and water, and then I gave them this little talk. I said, "I knew you had to come from a distance and I thought you would be willing to make final preparation here. I like the feeling of getting ready for the Communion." I lined them up, and one after another they "got ready" for the Communion. Well, a physical washing of your hands can be symbolic of the other kind of cleansing that ought to take place not only in the heart of a minister who is going to serve Communion, but in the hearts of the people who are going to take it. We must have clean hands and, more than that, we must have a clean heart. "Let us draw near with a true heart in full assurance of faith."

And the last scripture passage is in the book of James, in the fourth chapter. "Draw nigh to God, and he will draw nigh to you." How true that is! And that's the basis for the thing I want to say now. It's a two-way appeal. God calls us, and then we call God! When you start toward him, he starts toward you. The person who draws near to God knows right away that he can depend on God coming his way. The best picture of that is the story of the prodigal son and the old father. You can almost see the father looking down the road. As the boy decides to come home, the father doesn't wait for him to get there, but gets up and starts toward him. Every time a person sincerely starts toward God, you can depend upon it that God is already on his way to the lonely heart.

There are theologians who are trying to make out that God is hard to reach; that he's remote, austere; that there's something about his nature completely different from the nature of man; that we have no idea how repellent sin is and we have no notion how far removed we are, or what a great gulf is fixed between God and man. This is an emphasis that is needed—a kind of antidote to the theology we have had for the past twenty-five years. God has been pictured as a man lifted a little higher. He was thought of not only as benevolent and kind, but as indulgent. We all are a little bad, this reasoning goes. There is "a lot of good in the worst of us, and a lot of bad in the best of us." A sterner theology came as a natural reaction, but it's about time for someone to declare again that God cares and that God is a loving and forgiving God.

Many people feel that if there is a God, he must be so high and lifted up and so completely away from us that there isn't much chance for us. This isn't the New Testament idea: it certainly isn't the idea of Christ. The New Testament is a love story. It's God trying to find us. Just as soon as we start, he starts. He can do no more than that; there's no short cut. It requires a willing heart. We must have a hunger and thirst after righteousness, but just as soon as we are hungry or thirsty for righteousness, righteousness comes. I don't know of anybody in the world who ever sought and didn't find, or who knocked and to whom it was not opened. It's the true story of our faith, that as soon as we seek, he's there. God comes to us when we come to him. This whole exhortation to "draw near" means when we draw near, he draws near. One of the songs we love to sing around the altar contains these lines: "Though sundered far, by faith they meet around one common mercy-seat." It does seem that a miracle happens. It's a wonderful experience. We remember that when we come for Communion, God himself comes too. Not only that, but there's a coming together of kindred spirits. You find yourselves coming together as a family of God, communing. God draws near. We draw near. And then comes this wonderful experience of Communion.

Draw near with faith! That's the next part of the invitation. Does faith have something to do with drawing near to God? It has a lot to do with it. Can you really draw near to God without faith? I think we can *appear* to be drawing near. We can travel part of the road and go through the performance, but we never really draw near to God until we come in faith, believing.

That word "faith" doesn't mean what the boy said: "Believing what you know ain't so." Faith is a venture of the spirit. Faith is resting on the eternal arms. Faith is the outreach of your own heart toward the unseen, which being unseen belongs to the Eternal. Kirsopp Lake, many years ago, said, "Faith is not belief in spite of evidence, but it's life in scorn of consequence." In other words, you live as though you believed it true, and you scorn the results. And there are many who live this way. That is, they are in scorn of the consequence. They are like Job, who said, "Though he slay me, yet will I trust in him."

When we draw near with faith, a miracle takes place. I can't hope to explain to a person who has never had any such experience what this can mean. We come penitent, we come with love and charity for our neighbors, and we declare our intention of living a new life. And as we draw near to God, he draws near to us. We come into one of those wonderful experiences. We are not worried about definitions or concerned about the proper theological approach. It's like drawing near to your old home town on Thanksgiving or Christmas. The family have gathered together again, and there is warmth and wonder in the home-coming. There is security inside the walls of the old house, and you are with your friends.

On the other hand, it may be like the realizing of a dream, as for instance, when Mrs. Goff and I saw the Taj Mahal. We knew it was going to be quite a trip even from Delhi—a hot tiresome trip—but as we began to get near Agra we were all excited. We had to drive along a winding road, but we saw that the trees were a little thicker and the grass was cared for a little better, so we knew we were getting nearer and nearer. I kept my eyes shut for the last few moments. The dream was about to become reality. The Taj Mahal is the world's most beautiful building, and we were drawing near. Finally we made the last turn. The car stopped, and I looked up. There it was—the Taj Mahal —white marble set with thousands on thousands of semi-precious stones, glistening in the sunlight of that noonday. There were reflecting pools in front. I got right out and started toward the building. The guide started explaining this and explaining that. But not for me! The guide felt we should see the museum first—but no. I started for the Taj Mahal as if it were a magnet. The thing was of such exquisite beauty that I wanted to get nearer and nearer. I wasn't satisfied until I got right up to the stones, and finally, to the place where I could walk through the arches and into the very center of the world's most beautiful building.

I remember drawing near to the little town of Bethlehem. I will never forget drawing near to the Mount of Olives, or to the Garden of Gethsemane, or to the hill called Calvary. It is something like that when we draw near with faith. Don't ever think of the Communion as a commonplace experience. Don't ever approach the Lord's table in a casual manner. We are to approach the experience in wonder and awe. We know there is something real about this. As we go toward the Holy Communion, it seems to move toward us. The Taj Mahal couldn't move toward me. Our old home couldn't move toward me, and these sacred places in Palestine couldn't get up and come in my direction; but when I come to the altar of God, it's almost as though it comes toward me. And some people seem to meet it coming. That is, there is a commerce between their heart and the heart of God. They have drawn near with faith. They are now aware of the mystery. When one's heart meets the heart of God,

58

something begins to happen. These are things that are hard to explain, but are possible to experience, and the miracle is enacted over and over again.

No wonder that this one act has remained central in the Christian church for so long. No wonder that nearly every branch of the Christian church uses it in one form or another. No wonder we're referred to, not just as members, but as communicants. And no wonder there is a pull on the human heart when it's time to commune. By drawing near with faith we feel we are entering into a strange mystery. I've tried when I've been alone, to see if there is the same mystery about it. I've been in the church when there was not another soul there. I've prayed the prayer of consecration with nobody listening, and I found myself aware of the presence of God just as much as if someone were present. This is one worship experience that doesn't require an audience. It certainly doesn't depend on numbers. A packed house does not necessarily increase its meaning. More people can be brought under its spell, but it isn't dependent upon a crowd.

As we enter into the mystery of the service, we are close to the center of our faith. I can't believe that Jesus intended, in the first Communion, to initiate a kind of magical rite. I can't think that on an altar God is "made and eaten," as Browning's poem "The Bishop . . ." puts it. I can't think that we are able to work some miracle by our liturgy or that we can do away with our sins by magic, but in a spiritual sense we come close to the center of God's great way of speaking to a human heart. So the invitation to commune is "Draw near with faith."

I was preaching one night to a group of preachers in the mountains of Pennsylvania in a big theaterlike room. There were many empty seats near the front. Preachers are just as likely to sit far back as anyone else. They figure that if it isn't very good they can slip out. Since I found it was quite a distance to the people, I insisted that they come forward. "I don't want to embarrass you and I don't want to make you feel that you're under an obligation, but I just can't talk until I can get you here." I felt that they would have to "draw near," or I could not speak to them out of my heart.

Feeling that way, I can also see how God must want to get us near to him if he is to meet us in the Communion service. A man told me this story: "After my father died and we returned from the cemetery, my mother called us all into the 'front room.' [I suppose the room was used only on state occasions.] There were four boys, and I can never forget my mother saying, 'Get together, boys; get together.' And with us in a little circle she made her brave speech. 'Now, I don't know how we're going to make it, but I want you boys to stay with me and help me. We have the farm to pay for, and I can't do it alone.' As we stood in this little huddle, the boys got their arms around mother—she in the center —and said, 'We'll stay with you, mother.' That little scene," he said, "I've never forgotten." You see, she wanted them to draw near and they, in turn, wanted her with them. They had something to do together.

To come back to my Pennsylvania preachers—do you suppose God feels as I felt, only a million times more? I didn't want to talk to a few critical people who, with pencil and notebook, were trying to find out whether I said the thing in the proper way or not. I wanted to talk to the hearts of a group of preachers who were just as needy as I was. We were all sojourners on the way of life and needed each other. In my own church over and over again, a miracle has happened, when we seemed to become a united people, as though we were being drawn together. It is then that we are changed from a crowd into a worshiping congregation. And although we are together for only an hour, there is something about that bringing of souls together, especially under the awe and wonder of worship, that makes us *one*. It is not too much to believe that, after such an experience, we are never quite the same again. We know that people who are here for only an hour of that kind never forget it. Well, there's something like that about the Holy Communion. That's why Christ said, "Draw near and I will draw near to you." That's why the invitation to commune includes these wonderful words— "Draw near with faith." And as we come in faith, God meets us there. "Heaven comes down our souls to greet, and glory crowns the mercy seat." The experience of redemption is wrought, all over again, in these poor hearts of ours. It's a wonderful invitation. No part of it is more important than this little phrase: "Draw near with faith."

# SIX

# On Taking the Sacrament

THERE was a time when the sacramental service did not mean much to me. My earliest recollection of a Communion service was one of trembling and fear. Later I developed an indifference toward it. The service seemed strange. No one ever explained it to me. Later on it seemed that it didn't "belong." And for years I had difficulty in making it seem real. During the first years of my ministry I came to a better appreciation of its significance. I remember reading Dean Sperry's book *Reality in Worship* and the impression it made on me. It was then that the Communion service began to come alive.

Now let us think on this theme, "Taking the Sacrament," which means the act of Communion. Over and over, reference is made to the Communion as the Eucharist. The word "Eucharist," so far as I can discover, means "thanksgiving"—at least that is its central meaning. Some people would question this interpretation. They would make it into something different, but thanksgiving is an important part of the service, and was an important part of early Christian worship. The word "Communion" is also used. All of us know what it is to commune. The word "communist," with the same root, means sharing together. What we have in Russia is not communism. True communism is a rather wonderful thing if you think of it in the Christian sense. The early Christians shared things together. The plan wasn't entirely practical and it didn't seem to work for very long. But they actually shared their property—they shared everything in common for a while. That is, they shared according to need, each contributing for the good of the whole. They discovered quite early that this ideal was nearly impossible to achieve. But the church never gave up the idea of a spiritual sharing. And that idea is still alive and a real part of the Communion service until this day.

Another common interpretation of the Lord's Supper is that of sharing a simple meal. My own belief is that the first Communion was as simple as that. Christ and his disciples ate a meal together. Then came his breaking of bread. I imagine he took bread—a staple, a fundamental food—and held it up as though to say, "This is what you'll always be doing, since bread is so essential." In effect, he was saying, "Every time you break bread you will be reminded of my own broken body." Now remember, this was before the Crucifixion and is in anticipation of what was yet to come.

I've tried to think of some of the deep meanings of the act of Communion. I've tried to ask myself—How shall I prepare for Communion? I've tried to face this out to the best of my ability. I hope that what I am saying will be helpful to you as you commune. What should a person be thinking about as he approaches the Communion? What is the Christian teaching about it? Surely the service is a remembrance, for Christ said repeatedly, "This do in remembrance . . ." And so from the beginning the disciples thought of it as a memorial.

There was an advertisement for monuments in a recent magazine. It was beautifully done, although it dealt with a grim subject. It pictured a grassy plot and a stone and a little girl putting a bouquet of flowers on the grass. And then someone had written this caption, "No one is dead so long as he is remembered by someone." I could imagine the girl was thinking of her daddy as she placed the flowers on the plot of grass. In a far more wonderful way you are trying to memorialize Christ every time you make a trip to the altar. Every time you take a cup in your hand, every time you break bread, you have a symbol of remembrance and are reminded of that first Communion. And Christ is never dead so long as he is remembered. So it seems clear that one of the purposes of Communion is to keep Christ alive in memory. This was exactly what Jesus was doing—performing a simple act and asking people to repeat it through the centuries, using materials that would be universal, and then saying, "As oft as ye do this, do it in remembrance of me."

I do not think that in the Communion one ought to be thinking only of the death of Christ. It is a remembering of both his death and his life. When I start to take Communion, I often try to see the hill called Calvary in my imagination. Sometimes the thought of sorrow and suffering comes into my mind with great force. I seem to see him looking at the people and saying, "Father, forgive them; they don't know what they're doing." Sometimes I am overwhelmed by his love revealed to the thief on the cross. I seem to see the scene again. One of the thieves is berating him, while the other, apparently captured by Christ, is saying, "Lord, remember me when you come into your kingdom." And Jesus replies, "To day shalt thou be with me in paradise." I think of those things when I start communing. I try to think of a room, where a group of Christians gathered together for the last time. I don't think of a beautiful altar, alabaster cups, swinging censers, gold crosses, or rich vestments. We've added these things through the centuries. I like to think of a group of people sitting —not at a table as we think of it, not like Da Vinci's "Last Supper"—but seated as they were in that day and breaking bread together. When I think of those things, that's remembrance.

But now let us turn to the matter of thanksgiving, which is such a real part of Communion. When a minister distributes the elements, he will often say, following the words of the service, "Eat this in remembrance that Christ died for you, and feed on him in your heart by faith, with thanksgiving." And on taking the cup we hear the words, "Drink this in remembrance that Christ died for you, and be thankful." Over and over, that sentence is repeated. And why? For fear we may forget that Communion is thanksgiving. In the early church there was much thanksgiving. In the second chapter of Acts we read that they broke bread with gladness and singleness of heart. Yet get a feeling as you read these early stories that Communion in the early church was a radiant thing. When these people got together for Communion, they had the sense of thankfulness that transcended everything. Whether they were in the catacombs, or in somebody's house, they felt this sense of gratitude.

Those early church meetings where just a little handful gathered together were filled with praise and thanksgiving. What did these people have to be thankful for? They didn't have a ranch-type house and two cars. They didn't have an assured income. They didn't have wonder drugs. They had no social security, no pensions, no expectation of a ripe old age of happiness. But they had Christ, and a radiance was in their hearts. They had seen Christ, or if they hadn't seen him directly, they had seen some who had, and the story was transmitted from one to another. You can't read the story of the Christian church —the early church—without sensing this radiance. If that lost radiance should return and should come alive in us, there are enough Christians today to change the very climate. Think of the way the faith advanced—first in Asia Minor and then in Rome. The whole thing happened in those first years, moving steadily on until it captured the whole Roman Empire. And this thankfulness, this radiance, was at the heart of it.

What were the early Christians thankful for? Why, they had been forgiven. They had found a way to live. They were thankful for Christ, thankful for hope, thankful for redemption— and all of that in a dismal world. It is hard to believe. Certainly that optimism and that radiance ought not to be forgotten. When you come to the altar, it's not just to mourn. Sometimes you feel like weeping, but don't leave out thankfulness. So when you kneel to take the cup, start with, "O God, I'm so thankful— thankful that I'm able to be here, thankful for the mercies that have come to me, thankful that you've been so good, that I have so much, that I have a chance yet to serve. Let those things crowd into your mind. Some people have left thankfulness out of their prayers altogether. They're never thankful. All their prayers are just "Give me this," "Give me that," "Give me something else"—no gratitude, no sense of outgoing. It's all asking. If we took an honest test and told the truth, I wonder if we would not have to admit that most of our prayers are taken up with petition. We want things, so we pray for them. How little of thanksgiving to God for our blessings! I try, every night before I go to sleep, to say over and over to my own heart, and to God, how grateful I am. I can't count all my blessings. I just know I have more than I can enumerate. Come, then, to God with a grateful heart and with thanksgiving, because thanksgiving is a great part of the Christian faith. It begins right at the altar in Communion. So come to remember Christ. Come to be thankful.

Then there is something in the Communion about covenant, "I will make a new covenant with you." There are phrases in the service about "the covenant in my blood." What is a covenant? The ancient Jew knew about it. He made a covenant with God, and God made a covenant with him. God led the Jews out of the land of bondage. He gave to them the Commandments and he started them on the way to the Promised Land. And it was because God had made a covenant. There came a time when the covenant was broken. Even the temple was torn down, and old Jerusalem was ground to powder, but this promise, "I will make a new covenant," was always in the mind of the Jews. Jesus took the symbol of the old covenant—the broken one—and said, "I'll make a new covenant with you." That's the feeling that comes over us when we take Communion. You covenant with God. He covenants with you. And you now become a part of a solemn compact between your soul and the soul of God. That sense of a covenant is still with us. A covenant sealed by the shedding of blood. When we come to commune, the sense of covenant is there. It's the making over again of a new promise. You promise God obedience, and his promises are fulfilled in your heart even as you do it.

Another feeling that ought to come over us is the sense of fellowship. While Warner Sallman, the artist, was visiting with me, I said to him, "Warner, this is a great fellowship! Remember the old song, 'What a fellowship, what a joy divine'?" He replied, "Yes, it is wonderful that we can get together and share this feeling." You know how you feel when you meet somebody you haven't seen for a long time. In ordinary conversation with a friend we have many interesting things to talk about. But lift it to a higher plane, and think of a chance to talk to God, and you can see the wonder in such fellowship. How much there is to go over! Warner Sallman and I recalled how we first saw each other. I remembered him as a young artist sitting in a seat in front of me while I taught a Bible class. I recalled how we ate lunch once or twice together, and I remembered how we talked in other days, before his picture "Head of Christ" became so famous. And here we were still having fellowship.

Sometimes Christian fellowship reaches across the country; sometimes it reaches across the world. When my Buddhist friend, a Japanese professor whom I baptized several years ago, met me in Tokyo and took me around to meet his friends, he would always say, "He's my father." I think, of course, he meant "father in the gospel." I had fellowship with him, for we had something in common. I had placed my hand on his head and had said these words, "I baptize thee in the name of the Father, and the Son, and the Holy Spirit." It wouldn't make any difference now how far apart we were; nothing could really break that fellowship.

When the war was about to break out in Japan, and a group of missionaries were leaving the country, they met with a group of loyal Japanese Christians. Those people took a vow that no matter what happened, how serious the war, they would never, never give up their fellowship. Each had a little medal, or token, to carry away from that compact. I talked to one of these missionaries who had returned to Japan after the war. The members of the group who were left, he said, had a meeting. The terrible devastation of war had reduced their number, but those who could get back met again and sensed the wonder of a fellowship that was never broken.

There's another ·concept in Communion. It is nourishment. "Feed on him in your heart" is the ancient phrase. How can I tell a person to do that? Of course, it is only a suggestion—a reminder. It's something that you do inwardly. There is no physical expression of it that makes it any clearer than the words themselves. There is a hunger of the soul which can never be satisfied except in a spiritual way.

> Now the frail vessel Thou hast made
>     No hand but thine shall fill;
> For the waters of the earth have failed,
>     And I am thirsty still.

So with the hunger of the heart. What a wonderful promise in the Bible, "Blessed are they which do hunger and thirst after righteousness: for they shall be filled."

Another element in the Communion that "causes me to tremble" is the thought of atonement. Some have felt that the word means "at-one-ment." Of course, there is something like that in atonement. We become one, but I don't think that's a very profound observation. The atonement is greater than "at-one-ment." The atonement is the innocent suffering for the guilty, and when you come in the presence of the atonement, you stand on the edge of a mystery.

Have you ever seen the ocean—the Atlantic or the Pacific? What did you really see? My first view of the Pacific was disappointing. Of course, they said to me, "This is only the sound at Seattle." But I wasn't satisfied with that, not until I saw the ocean. But you nearly always see the ocean from a bay or a sound or an inlet or a cove, just some little indentation of the land. I have seen the ocean right out from the rocky coast, a boundless ocean with no visible distant shore. But can you really see the ocean? Nobody who knows the ocean would agree that you'd seen it until you have been on it. On a fast ocean liner you can go across it in four days, and you think you've seen it. But the boat is so big that the feel of the ocean is never quite as real as it is when you are on a smaller one. I once rode on a smaller boat for ten days. The boat was moved about in the trough of the wave—up high, back and forth. That was something! But you never really see the ocean until you are out on it alone, maybe alone on a raft as some have been.

A magazine article told of a couple who sought to cross the Atlantic in a sailboat. They sailed into a great storm. One night the young husband went aloft to take in a sail. His wife was below with her baby. She heard the sound of the wind and felt the tossing of the boat, and finally when he did not come back, she decided he had been thrown into the sea. She was helpless and alone. Minutes seemed like hours. There was nothing at all she could do about it except to hope and pray. At last he returned and they weathered the storm. The magazine article made that experience live. I am sure this couple found out what the ocean is like, but to stand on the shore and look at it you wouldn't know —not unless you had been in a storm and had had some contact with the ocean in its fury. You'll never really know the ocean until you live with it.

It's much the same with this mystery of Communion. As you come to the cross you may think of the death of Christ and of his redemption, but you may be able to see it only as forgiveness, or you may see it as a manifestation of the love of God. In such times you seem to hear a cry from it. It's a startling thing, like lightning across the sky. The atonement, redemption—all of that is in the Communion.

"This is my body." Is it a miracle? Is this a sacrifice that's re-enacted always to remind God that he is a redeemer? I can't believe that. The word "mass" comes from the word *missare*. At first it meant only "to send." In the early church it meant that when the people finished the regular service and were about to have Communion, they would send out all those who weren't really baptized and were not regular members. I doubt whether at first it meant anything more than that dismissal. We have no record of its being used until the third century, but think of all the things that have been included in the meaning of the word. It is unfortunate that the service has so often taken on the form of magic. To suppose that we could create on an altar a miracle of that sort, or that the repeating of the miracle on the altar is just to remind God of his obligation, is a very strange interpretation. The idea of the mass, with these magical elements, is something that the Protestant cannot accept because he does not believe that God has to be appeased or that God has to be placated. How any priest or minister could suppose that he himself could bring about such a miracle is beyond me. God does not need to be reminded of his promise or of the sacrifice he has made. The ancient church of Ethiopia has in its Communion the sense of the renewing of a covenant. This seems a far better interpretation.

I can remember in my boyhood we used to have what was called a "love feast." Bread and water were used. I used to go with my mother to that little love feast. It was usually preceded by a testimony meeting. It was a wonderful experience. Here were these few Christians holding a service, and in the intimacy of that fellowship they would try to tell of their progress or failures. The love feast was held only once or twice a year. It was the most intimate and sacred service that I knew. Many people from the outside couldn't understand it, but they weren't supposed to. It gave to these Christians the sense of being bound together.

Well, these are all just glimpses into this mystery and the wonder of what happens as we commune. And so whether you take this as a remembrance, or as a thanksgiving, or as a covenant, or as a fellowship such as I have described, you will still not fully understand or encompass the nature of the Lord's Supper. And you will still have only a part of the total meaning.

On taking the Communion, we must come in a penitent mood, searching our hearts for wrong. We must come trying to see whether we measure up to the standards of Christ. And as we come he lives again in our remembrance. He isn't just a Christ on a cross, but he is in our lives.

A little girl, seeing an empty cross, asked, "Jesus isn't on that cross, is he?" Some who heard it might have agreed that there was something lacking. But that's the wonder of the empty cross. That's the glory of it—Jesus isn't on it. He isn't on any cross. He *was* on a cross, and that sacrifice and that redemption were once and for all. But thank God he is alive! And so, Communion means a living Christ—in your room, in your heart, to follow you in the nighttime, to be with you in the morning, to be with you now and forever.

Is there any act in all the world that is so significant? Is there anything that could compare with this—the taking of a little piece of bread? I don't blame people for saying that it is difficult. I've had people in all sincerity say to me that it was a hindrance —the use of any physical thing. And I know that it's difficult to use material objects like bread and wine. "It gets in the way," they say. And I know that it could. But go a little further; take the next step. After all, we are using symbols, and much of our world is described by symbols that are as physical as bread and wine. And so we take these simple elements as symbols of something far greater.

I hope the wonder of the Holy Communion will never, never leave you. I hope none of us will ever come to a Communion without a sense of awe and with some hesitation. I wish it were possible for people to come to Communion whenever they felt like it, and I wish they could stay as long as they desired. Because of limiting conditions we can't do it that way, but we can at least make our own pilgrimage in our own way. The journey from the seat to the altar becomes for each one of us a kind of glorified journey. We enter again with Christ into the holiest thing that we know anything about in this world. "Take this holy Sacrament to your comfort; and devoutly kneeling make your humble confession to Almighty God."

I found in a little book a few words which I want to conclude with. They're written by Jeremy Taylor, who wrote a book called *Holy Living,* and another entitled *Holy Dying.* The latter greatly influenced John Wesley. It was this little book that Wesley said changed his life. The book I got in England was dated 1739. That's pretty old for a book. When I went through it I wondered why it could ever have so influenced John Wesley. So much was said about dying. Yet that was the thing that stirred Wesley.

Here is the substance of Jeremy Taylor's words about taking the Holy Communion.

When you awake in the morning of your communion day, give thanks to God, particularly that He has blessed the opportunity for your receiving the symbols of pardon, the sacrament of Christ Himself, the seal of immortality. Hasten early out of your bed. The cock crowing that morning is like the noise that is made by the coming of the bridegroom. And, therefore, go out to meet Him. . . . Make a general confession of your sin and be very much humbled in the sense and appreciation of worshiping Jesus. Love Him, dedicate yourself to Him. Recollect what He has done for thy soul, what mysteries He has appointed, and by what ministries He conveys Himself to you. When thou seest a holy man, dispute no more; inquire no more; doubt no more; be divided no more. But believe and with the eyes of faith and of the spirit thou seest Christ's body broken on a cross. Thou seest Him bleeding for your sins. Thou feedest upon the food for elect souls. And when thou dost receive thy Lord, do thou also receive thy brother into thy heart. After you have given thanks and have finished your private and public devotions, go home. Do not presently forget this solemnity and sink from the sublimity of devotion and mystery into some secular conversation like a falling star from brightness down into dirt. What we may do by devotion and solemn religion that day, we must do every day by the material practice of virtues.

So said Jeremy Taylor in describing "The worthy communicant." It is a high standard but not too high when we face God's altar.

# SEVEN

### ✹

## *To Your Comfort*

WE TURN now to the consideration of this phrase: "to your comfort." I have discussed Repentance, the Neighbor, the Great Intention, Walking in His Holy Way, Drawing Near with Faith, Taking the Sacrament, and now, To Your Comfort.

What is the first thing that comes to your mind when someone mentions the word "comfort"? For moderns the word is very likely connected with physical or creature comforts. So many things are being done for our comfort. We're warmed when it's cold, air-conditioned when it gets hot. We are fed when we are hungry; we're transported to work and back; and we have all manner of conveniences, all manner of gadgets to make life comfortable. We have drugs to relieve our pain—any number of things surrounding us from morning until night just to make us comfortable. I haven't anything against that. I'm as anxious for comfort as you are. I am sure I give a great deal of attention to trying to be comfortable. I think most everyone does the same. In America today we are spending sums utterly unbelievable for comfort, and they tell us we're just on the edge of new things that will be coming—the houses that will be kept at the same temperature all year . . . the multitude of devices, labor-saving and others—all for our comfort. But I wouldn't need to tell you, would I, that this isn't the kind of comfort we're talking about when we come to commune?

The word "comfort" actually means a sense of well-being. It has reference to a calm and serene outlook on life. It certainly means more than just the absence of pain. Perhaps the lowest meaning of comfort would be this material well-being—the creature comforts that I've mentioned.

Although the Bible uses this word so frequently, when I turn to the hymnbook to find hymns on comfort, there is no selection at all. There's not one hymn listed under that word "comfort," and yet it's so much a part of our Christian faith. But the word, in the Bible, has a variety of meanings. I went through the Bible carefully and I think at least 135 times this word is used directly, to say nothing of its synonyms. That's a lot of times, for there are some words that you think are very popular that aren't used more than a dozen times.

"Comfort" is a word found in both the Old and New Testaments, and I've tried to group the verses in which it occurs to see how the meanings compare. I've grouped them under four headings. I'll not give you all the locations, but the first meaning might be called "support." Comfort means support; that is, means something to make us strong, to hold us up. One of the great prayers of the Church contains this word "support": "O Lord, support us all the day long . . . , until the shadows lengthen, and the evening comes, and the busy world is hushed, and the fever of life is over." That prayer, old as it is, and used so often, has been a most helpful one. For many a soul it has been, more than anything else, just the prayer to express the deepest need.

76

Well, that's one of the meanings of "comfort" in the Bible. Remember the twenty-third psalm, "Thy rod and thy staff they *comfort* me"—they *support* me.

In another group of verses the word takes on a different meaning—comfort means helpful companionship. You get this meaning in Isaiah and in many other places. "Comfort ye, comfort ye my people, saith your God." Can't you hear that in an anthem? And doesn't it haunt you? Haven't you ever felt that way when you opened the Bible, or when you entered into some spiritual experience? Comfort seemed to be so necessary. It became the wistful cry of your soul. "O God, comfort me." And we mean by that, "Help me. I must have healing; I must have help; I must have someone to aid me."

We find the same idea in the Gospel of John, in which we are told that "the Comforter will come." Jesus said, "It's better for you that I go away, but if I go I will send the Comforter." And the word there really means just that. The Comforter, the paraclete, the one that goes alongside to help, to aid—it's as though you had a companion. And what Christian has not felt the need for companionship in some dark hour or in some lonely experience? "Oh for the touch of a vanished hand," we say. Oh, for the feeling that there is someone who can walk along with you, one who will not leave you alone. And that, I think, is the way the word is used in Isaiah.

Now there is another meaning of "comfort" in the book of Lamentations. You can imagine this book would be filled with this word—"consolation." Over and again it is used there, and, of course, the author of Lamentations was lamenting the fact that he hadn't anyone to comfort him. The sentence "I sigh: there is none to comfort me" is in the first chapter of the book. The word

77

means to be cheered—it means to be gladdened. And we need to be cheered up. In one of our hymns we use the phrase "Cheer this sad heart of mine." I've heard congregations sing it, and sing it as if they really meant it. How many times I have sung a hymn like that!

I have been in a church, worshiping with others, when it seemed to me that I needed cheering up almost more than anything else. I remember one morning going into a church in lower Manhattan in New York, old John Street Church. I was so lonely that morning. I didn't know anybody, but I found a little group of people there on this hot Sunday morning. I heard the music before opening the door. I was late; I had taken a taxi and the man couldn't find the church. He had driven round and round, finally stopping at 44 John Street ready to give up, and there we were! When I got out of the cab I could hear the congregation singing. I thought they were singing "Blest Be the Tie That Binds." When I got inside I found it was the same tune, but the words were different. I can still feel the sense of wonder as I stood with this little congregation of strangers. I felt at one with them. We were singing a song of cheer. It was a song intended to affirm that we were not alone. It had exactly this same idea about it.

> Why should this anxious load
> Press down your weary mind?
> Haste to your heavenly Father's throne,
> And sweet refreshment find.

Now for the fourth meaning of this word. "Comfort," in the Bible, sometimes means "release" or "relief." This is the meaning in the New Testament over and over again. In Second Corinthians, the first chapter, the word appears in three verses. Paul used that word ten times—comfort, comfort, comfort. It did not always have the same meaning. There are different shadings, but Paul uses the word throughout all his epistles. He writes, "That ye may be comforted—by the comfort that is in the gospel." What he really means is that the believer will get *relief* and release, and that's what we need. Think of the increase in mental distress. It's hard to tell the difference between those who are the happiest and those who are carrying the heaviest load because people put on a front. They try to bluff it out, and I don't blame them. Very few people wear their feelings on their sleeves. Every now and again a letter comes to my desk, or a telephone call. Somebody will pull back the curtain a bit and will let me have a look, and then I'll know. Sometimes when I talk to people in the study, or in a quiet place, they let me have a look into their lives; and I've often seen a lonely heart even though everything on the outside seemed to be wonderful. There are people who just radiate happiness and never reveal their deep feelings: the deep loneliness, the deep hurt, or the great hunger of their heart.

Well, Paul bases his whole gospel on this word "comfort." It's just as though he were saying, "There is relief from mental distress." You can find freedom; you can have peace of mind and peace of soul. There is help . . . there is a balm in Gilead . . . there is hope for the sin-sick soul. All of this is involved in that word "comfort." Jesus said, "I will not leave you comfortless." Now doesn't that mean a lot? He's promised not to leave his people without the aid of great comfort. So, "to your comfort" means "for your support, your help, your consolation, your relief." All these things, I think, are involved. To change the language

79

a little bit—comfort means to make strong or strengthen. It means to aid and help. It means to cheer and gladden. It means to relieve from distress and weariness. One hymn which we use during the Communion service has these lines:

> Here, O my Lord, I see Thee face to face;
> Here would I touch and handle things unseen,
> Here grasp with firmer hand eternal grace,
> And all my weariness upon Thee lean.

And so I think that's one of the clear meanings of this word.

There's another meaning in this word "comfort." We occasionally talk about words themselves as being "comfortable." We have this expression in some of our Communion services—"the comfortable word." Such words have healing in them. Sometimes people use them when they want to say more than they could any other way. They use these words in times of sorrow. The words give us a sense of oneness. No wonder then we are told that a few words "fitly" chosen are like apples of gold in pictures of silver. Such words are comfortable indeed. And with these words we take the Sacrament.

In the long history of the church there have been many views of the Sacrament. Sometimes it has been thought of as magic. Some have thought of the Sacrament in materialistic terms. They felt it was something important to their physical well-being, and they received it, believing that it might work a miracle. Some have thought of it as a sacrifice, as though Christ had been offered on the altar and had become a substitution for their sins. This has been a profound belief of the church. It has had a variety of interpretations. I like to think that it has many facets. You cannot explain the Sacrament in one sentence. Turn it and look at it, and seeing its many sides you may feel that you will never be able to describe it adequately. But the comfortable word, the healing word, the supporting word, the word of consolation, and the word of relief—all these are included in the phrase "and take this holy Sacrament to your comfort."

So when you take Communion think of it in this new sense, the sense of comfort. When you arise to go, may the comfort of God go with you. May you feel that someone is going along by your side, healing your hurts. May you realize that there is indeed a balm in Gilead which can heal the sin-sick soul. May your next Communion have a special meaning for your own trouble, and your own heartache, and your own sin. It is a comfortable gospel. Not comfort as we ordinarily think of it, but something that gives us a sense of peace and a confidence that all is well.

Do you remember the old song "The Comforter Has Come"? I haven't heard it in years. I can still hear it. We used to sing it in that little Iowa church, "Oh spread the tidings round wherever man is found, the Comforter has come." I didn't know then what it meant. I was very young, but I listened. What strange notions a hymn can generate! I joined with the little congregation as they sang it, announcing with joy, "The Comforter has come." But I was thinking of comfort just as I experienced it. We didn't have electric blankets, but we did have "comforters." There were one or two of them that were special. If we ever got sick, out would come a comforter. And how wonderful it was to have mother tuck it around us! There was something special in that. One night I remember I was so sick I couldn't tell where I was. It seemed that the ceiling of the room was open to the sky. I didn't realize that I had a raging fever, but I did know that mother had brought out the special comforter and that I was now the object of special interest. The comforter had come! And to me the song meant just that. It gave me the feeling that I was being cared for and that everything would be all right. In some such sense we feel the "comfort" in Communion. And you, fevered or suffering distress of heart . . . you who are lonely or feel you can't make it . . . you who wonder what the next step may be—you can know there is comfort in the Christian faith.

> I know not what the future hath
> Of marvel or surprise,
> Assured alone that life and death
> God's mercy underlies.

It's a great feeling to know that you do not walk alone. You can face the night and the morning with that kind of confidence. God's mercy does underlie all our lives. That's a real comfort.

The Passover was a joyful experience for devout Jews. The angel of death "passed over." It didn't stop at their house; there was blood on the lintel of the doorpost, and so the angel passed over. When the early disciples broke bread in their Communion service, they were thinking of the Passover too. And they had the same "comfortable" feeling. Jesus invested the service with new meaning—"As oft as ye do this, think of me." Perhaps he was saying, "Never break bread without thinking of me." "Never drink of the cup without thinking of me." I believe it started in that simple way. The church has made much more of it, and I think it's a good thing. If Christ were to come back on earth, I do not think he would condemn the variety of interpretations we make of the Communion, because it has become a part of the history of man's spiritual experience and of the wonder of our faith.

There are many symbols that go far beyond the thing itself. A flower pressed in a book may have a world of meaning to you, and mean nothing to someone else. I've got three little locks of hair put away. They are dated "1925." There were three little girls then. One was a blonde, another was dark, and a third was in between. There's so much more to those three little pieces of hair than you might appreciate. If you found them you would throw them out. Some of you know what it is to have a little shoe gilded. Some of you have a ring that has a very special meaning. These things are symbols; they have a far deeper meaning than the immediate article reveals. That's the way it is when you come to lift the cup. Forget that it's just a cup. Go beyond that to the deeper meaning. Go back to that first Communion—to that first Passover which was turned into a communion, into a fellowship.

No wonder Christians are called "communicants." I suppose you could be a Christian if you didn't commune. But the communicant is one who joins a long procession and, moving toward the cup and the piece of bread, realizes that he is seeking something more, and he must have this something more. That's why we commune. So take the Sacrament *to your comfort.*

# EIGHT

## The Humble Confession

"Confession is good for the soul." We hear that often, and certainly the modern emphasis on psychiatry, with its efforts to give people release, testifies that it is true. We are a strange lot today. Think of all the neurotics who have something that baffles them, the confused, the mentally upset. We are trying to find out why. But I am sure there is no one simple answer to that problem. It is like most other things in life. We will have to seek for a variety of answers.

Some time ago a woman from another town came to me. She said, "You know, if I were a Catholic I would go to my priest, but I simply can't go to a minister in our town and tell him what I have on my heart." Well, I have a good pair of ears and I told her to go ahead, that I could listen to anything because I had heard everything. Nobody shocks me much any more. So she went ahead and talked. When she got all through she admitted that her problem was not too difficult. But it did give her a sense of release to talk to someone about it, and I think it did her some good.

Well, that happens of course every day. I remember very well a certain woman who came to me and wouldn't give her name. She wouldn't tell me where she lived, but I heard a perfect torrent of things. She went on for about thirty minutes and I kept still. At the end of the thirty minutes she got up, took her pocketbook, and asked, "How much do I owe you?"

"You don't owe me anything."

"I want to pay my bill."

"No, we get paid other ways. You don't owe me anything."

She said, "But I would like to pay you. You'll never know how much you helped me this morning."

I guess she was right about that—I never would know because I didn't do anything. But she went out feeling better. I think she just wanted to unload. She told me what she thought of her husband and of his cruelty. That was one thing she didn't dare tell anyone else. I didn't know who he was and couldn't betray any confidences. Again I think she found release in opening her heart to another person.

I have already referred to the "class meeting" once held in Methodist churches. There were some aspects of it that I didn't like. The same things were often repeated over and over, but there was one wonderful thing about it. The people had a chance to open up their hearts in those little intimate meetings. There wouldn't be more than a dozen present. My mother used to sit there so scared! The leader called on everyone, and when he went down the line and your turn came, you were supposed to get up and say something. My mother dreaded it. I think it was an ordeal every Sunday. Yet she felt she ought to go. When they called on her she would get up and confess some shortcoming, about the same sort of thing each time.

But now and then someone would say something most interesting. He might start by asking others to pray for him and ask forgiveness because he had lost his temper or had done something he was ashamed of. Perhaps someone had said words he couldn't bring back, and he would ask the others to pray for him so he might never do it again. It was a kind of "confessional," and I think it did some good.

It did us good to hear other people talk, not always about their troubles or their sins, but sometimes about their successes. In sharing they were able to do a great deal for one another. Now that we Methodists have given it up, the method has been picked up by other churches. I am sorry we have made no place for it, for I think confession is almost essential for a human being. I don't know whether or not you think of this need to confess as important. It is not possible for one to bottle up all his innermost feelings and never express them in any way. So I think it is true that confession is good for the soul.

Recently I found an illustration of this thing's being badly handled. The writer called it "Mrs. Grundy's Sewing Circle," and he said it was really a sort of Protestant confession, where women got together and "confessed" the sins of their neighbors. That, of course, is still a common practice. In any office or in any organization anywhere, when groups get together they usually "confess" the other fellow's sins, as well as his faults and failures. Sometimes I have wondered how we survive, because we are so unkind to each other. It doesn't make much difference how pious the group is. I have even heard ministers attack another brother. If he lifts his head above the horizon, they begin to shoot at him then for sure. When someone is trying to do something worth while in the world, it is the tendency of some of us to try to bring him down to our level. Very often we have confessions of real jealousy, and that god is a green god. If we have confessed the other fellow's sins, we will try to detail all his faults. We will see to it that they are all dragged out. If there are any weaknesses, we will make sure that they are all portrayed.

It is a good thing we don't hear everything that people say about us. I don't think I want to hear too much. When I first visited my church in Chicago, I went to the station following the service and got on the train to return to my former parish. I sat down in the dining car. At the table just next to mine two men were sitting together, and one asked, "Did you go to church this morning?" The other one said, "Yes."

"Where did you go?"

"I went to the Chicago Temple."

The train had started to glide out of the station. The first man asked, "Who preached there?" The other fellow replied, "Some young fellow from another town." I stretched my ears as the first one asked, "What did you think of the sermon?" Just at that point the train went over the trestle, and I'll never know what that fellow said. I am almost glad I didn't hear it.

It is strange how we can talk about the other person when most of us need to talk about ourselves. We talk about our outer selves too much—the self we have got on parade, the person we think we are, or the one we would like to think we are, or the person we would like to be.

There are people who do their confessing in a sort of vicarious fashion. They pick up the other person's good qualities and they confess them. But I don't believe we need to confess the other fellow's sins—or his virtues. When we do that, we just pick up the other person's qualities and identify ourselves with him. We "become" that person. I think all of us are this way at times. I have seen a mother whose daughter was in love become a part of the situation herself. She begins to fall in love in a rather vicarious way. I have seen weddings in which you could hardly tell whether it was the girl or the mother who was getting married. The mother had accepted the situation and put herself into it. She identified herself with the girl's position. I don't think it is anything to be too critical about, but it illustrates the possibility of our becoming another person by that method.

I found out something about the negative side of vicarious confession during my early work in Chicago in a mission. On my first Sunday morning in Chicago I woke up in one of those "hotels" over on Madison Street—the wrong kind of place. I didn't know anything about Chicago. I was just a boy. I had brought all I owned in an old valise. Do you remember the kind they used to call telescopes? There was a reason for that. If you got any more worldly possessions, you just kept putting them in, and it would extend itself. All you needed was a bigger strap! I had arrived, carrying that old telescope down the street, and had asked a policeman for a hotel. He said, "Right there." The sign read "Beds, ten cents." I asked him to show me a better one and he showed me one where the beds were twenty-five cents. I sat on the edge of that bed all night! I wouldn't get into that thing. It was inhabited, and I prefer to sleep alone.

The next morning I went across the street to a rescue mission. A group of people was out on the street singing to some poor human derelicts. I got up and joined them and sang with them. Within two weeks I was their preacher. That is how I got into it. Of course, there was no salary. It is amazing how you can get a job when you don't get any pay for it. I didn't want any pay for it, but one of the things I found out about the rescue mission was the people did so much confessing. Sometimes I found men who were better than they claimed to be.

This is a sort of inverted hypocrisy. The men would get up and tell how bad they were. For instance, someone would say, "I want to say I have been selfish and the Lord saved me from selfishness." The next one would say, "I was both selfish and greedy," and another one would say, "I was selfish and greedy, but I began to steal and the Lord saved me from being a thief." The next one would tell us he was greedy and stole, but worse than that he used to get drunk. It wouldn't take very long before men actually confessed things that were not their own sins. They were confessing the other fellow's sins. They were identifying themselves with others. They were putting on an act. That is a strange kind of hypocrisy.

Do you know what a hypocrite is? It is a person who pretends to be better than he really is, but an inverted hypocrite is a person who pretends that he is worse than he really is. The movies and much literature today describe a type that I seldom meet. They imply that hypocrites are everywhere. They are referred to as bigoted reformers, dressed in black, with eyes set close together. Usually they carry an umbrella. They are forever poking their thin blue noses into other people's business. But those characters are not like the people I know.

I cannot find people anywhere who describe themselves as very good. If I start a conversation with a stranger and raise the question about church attendance, I will likely get some such reply as: "I am not much of a church person. I go once in a while because I like the music," or "My wife thinks I ought to go, so I go on rare occasions." We have more church members now than ever in our history—a great many more. Could it be that many of these supposedly indifferent people are really church-goers and actually better than they pretend to be?

I read a book recently that was written by a professor who ought to have known better. The whole book was an attack on the church. He was embittered. I suppose he would say that he was being creatively critical. But I don't think he was doing any good. I think he was doing damage because all the way through he was attacking something that was not real. He was training his siege guns on old ideas that had been abandoned long ago. He was fighting what he called hypocrisy. When you know the church, you know that the great sin is not the sin of hypocrisy in its older form. Our great sin is that we do not stand for anything much. The philosophy we live by seems to be, "There is a little bad in the best of us and a lot of good in the worst of us." It is hard to do much about that. Wouldn't it be a refreshing experience to have somebody stand up and say he believes intensely in *something?* I like to hear a positive message. If you love the church, why don't you say so? If it has been good to you, why don't you thank God for it?

When I think about what the church has done for me, I feel I must confess my positive belief in it. It put its arms around me when I was a boy, and every day from that time to this the church of Christ has been better to me than I could have expected. When it comes to the end I would not want them to say a lot of foolish things about me. But I want somebody to confess my faith for me, to tell how Christ won me as a boy and all through the years has helped me and blessed me, so that I could never repay a thousandth part of the debt I owe to him. Those would be true and sincere words, and they would be my confession. The church has been a mother and a father to me. It has been a shelter in the time of storm. It has been just about everything for me. I cannot easily endure unfair criticism of it.

In modern Protestantism much of our literature is critical. We have many people who can tell what is wrong with the church. But since we have more to be grateful for than to find fault with, we should confess our faith in the church to the world. If you have faith, let the world know it. If you have been helped, tell it—confess it. Put that candle on a candlestick. Lift that little light high, for it is a dark world and people need light.

Whenever you find human kindness, whenever you find anybody who is sacrificial, and whenever you find anybody who is forgiving, pick up the fact and emphasize it. Here is a good exercise. Find five things before tonight that you are thankful for or that you appreciate. Then tell of your appreciation. Witness to it. Confess it! It is amazing when you confess your faith. You not only confess something inside your own heart, but you awaken the dormant faith of others. We live somewhat by the faith of others. We catch faith. We are infected by goodness as well as by disease. When we confess our faith we do something for the timid ones. Confess your belief and other people will start confessing theirs. Most of us are surrounded with pessimisms, doubt, criticism, and constant faultfinding—there are people who live on it from morning until night. If we confess our faith, then somebody else begins to live by the light that we have.

At the same time we have to confess our sins. God knows that, and we ought to know it. We know that we cannot hide a thing from him. We know that we have to come clean. There isn't any way by which we can go two directions at the same time. How long can you keep on with a secret sin? You know that it inevitably has to be faced. None of us can hope to find the forgiveness that we want if we are not willing to open our hearts to God.

If we are really honest, we know that we have need—great need—for forgiveness. If I were going to try to build a moral order or to improve on the present one, I would retain the sense of guilt and the hunger for forgiveness. These are necessary to us as sinners. When we are utterly unaware of that need and go blissfully on our way, we are in the greatest danger and cannot know the joy of forgiveness. You know how a dog will look at you to see if you are going to forgive him? Even an animal senses this desire to be received back into fellowship. How much more so where human beings are concerned—when they have harmed each other and find themselves in need of forgiveness or have broken fellowship with God! Psychologists have correctly described our divided personalities when we are at war with ourselves. They have put it on a purely materialistic basis—often not on a Christian basis. It seems to me that it transcends anything of that kind. Have you known what it is to be torn and divided? All at 6's and 7's? At "odds" with yourself and the world? And have you then made your humble confession and found forgiveness? There is peace in forgiveness, something we cannot have in any other way. We are all like Paul in the book of Romans, battling with ourselves—"O wretched man that I am!" But in humble confession something happens!

Forgiveness is a wonderful experience. Some years ago in my class in college there was a young fellow who, according to all standards, was "going places." He really was a brilliant fellow and I think sometimes he outdid the professors with his embarrassing questions. He was just about as good as any student we had in school. Although he used to be very cynical and I thought many times the chief skeptic among us all, I was amazed later to find that he had registered at the seminary. I could hardly believe it when I heard it, and when I asked him, "How do you happen to be here?" he said, "Oh, I just wanted to find out a few things." And apparently, he found them out. Theology seemed to be his "happy hunting ground." He would explode a theory here and a theory there. I lost track of him until some time later, when I learned he had become secretary to a missionary bishop. In that relationship he went to India. That was fine—he could now see something of the world and write about it. One day I had a letter from him. It was worded in intellectual terms, to be sure, but he wrote of what had happened to him. He was given a job of writing about a religious revival that had broken out there. He said, "My own personality has been unified." (He meant he had been forgiven.) I know what happened! Christ got hold of his life. He saw himself a sinner in need of forgiveness, and for the first time made his humble confession. He was changed. He had made his peace with God. He was forgiven. O wonderful sense of forgiveness—have you no need of it? Is there any one of us who does not need to say, "O God, forgive!" Are we at the place where it has no appeal? God pity us if that is true!

Think of Peter when Jesus first met him. Do you remember when Peter fell on his face, right in the boat, and said, "Depart from me; for I am a sinful man, O Lord"? Someone has pictured another scene years later. Peter now is preaching the gospel of Christ and goes back and tells the story of what happened. "I stood there and he just looked at me, and I never really knew what he was like until he looked at me. He did not berate me. He just looked at me, and for the first time I really saw myself— my selfishness and my excuses. I could not look at him. I could not look at his face—and I just fell right down in the boat and said, 'Depart from me; for I am a sinful man, O Lord.'" I can imagine Peter continuing, "For the first time I realized there was such a thing as divine love in the world and that the one who was calling me was the lover of my soul. That is why I left my nets. He knew me better than I knew myself. That is why I followed him."

In humble confession you meet that divine love. Once it reaches you—into the very depths of you—you will know the meaning of Communion.

> O the pure delight of a single hour
> That before Thy throne I spend,
> When I kneel in prayer, and with Thee, my God,
> I commune as friend with friend!